D0387260

Jack Smith

Oct. 13, 1980

Jack Smith's

L.A.

Books by Jack Smith

JACK SMITH'S L.A.

SPEND ALL YOUR KISSES, MR. SMITH

THE BIG ORANGE

GOD AND MR. GOMEZ

SMITH ON WRY

THREE COINS IN THE BIRDBATH

Jack Smith's

by Jack Smith

McGRAW-HILL BOOK COMPANY

NEW YORK   ST. LOUIS   SAN FRANCISCO

DÜSSELDORF   MEXICO   TORONTO

1 2 3 4 5 6 7 8 9— DODO— 8 7 6 5 4 3 2 1 0

LIBRARY OF CONGRESS CATALOGING IN PUBLICATION DATA

Smith, Jack Clifford, 1916–
    Jack Smith's L.A.
    1. Los Angeles—Social life and customs—Addresses,
essays, lectures. 2. Los Angeles—Description—
Addresses, essays, lectures. I. Title.
F869.L85S57   979.4'94   80-13127
ISBN 0-07-058471-0

For Denise
It's her L.A. too

AUTHOR'S NOTE

These mostly affectionate reports and reflections on life in Los Angeles in the 1970s are drawn from the author's column in the *Los Angeles Times*. They are offered here without regard for chronology, and if the reader should encounter what appears to be an anachronism now and then, he is asked to enjoy it.

Contents

Foreword

No other city on earth attracts as many critical journalists as Los Angeles, but few of them seem to have much insight into this nondescript metropolis. Perhaps, as in the story of the elephant and the seven blind men, your idea of Los Angeles depends on which part of it you get hold of.

All writers, when they visit a city other than those with which they are familiar, are overcome by the Tocqueville syndrome—an irresistible urge to hurry home and get the place down on paper. When the city observed is Los Angeles, their articles usually have the tone of philippics rather than objective reports. One of the symptoms of the Tocqueville syndrome is that the visiting writer imagines himself endowed with a vision and insight that are quite lacking in the natives.

Most of the pieces I have read on Los Angeles in recent years appeared to be rewrites of pieces written by dyspeptic screenwriters in the 1930s, when the stars of the American literary scene were in the employ of Hollywood's unlettered nabobs and were out here lapping up our sunshine and our orange juice and vodka, and working off their shame and frustration by pecking out dispatches about our hideous architecture, our empty heads and our taste for the very trash they were being forced to write, in captivity.

Ironically, this peculiar genre was invented by Willard Huntington Wright, a long-ago literary editor of the *Los Angeles Times*, who later wrote the Philo Vance detective novels as S. S. Van Dyne. Back in 1913 Mr. Wright described Los Angeles as being settled by yokels from the Midwest—yokels who were "nourished by rural pieties and superstitions and had a righteous abhorrence of shapely legs, late dinners, malt liquors, grand opera and hussies." He added that the lights went out at midnight.

Ever since those words were published in *Smart Set* magazine Mr. Wright's rococo and sardonic style has been echoed, imitated and plagiarized by almost every journalist who has come this way. Oddly, though, the coin has been turned. We no longer are accused of piety, abstinence and righteousness, but of their opposites. No matter, the indictment is still delivered in the same tone of moral and intellectual superiority.

A decade after Mr. Wright came H. L. Mencken, the sage of Baltimore, who was the mentor of my own generation. Mr. Mencken made the obligatory trip to Los Angeles and observed that "the whole place stank of orange blossoms."

"When one hears of the place at all," he went on, "one hears that some citizen has been jailed for reading the Constitution of the United States, or that some new swami in a yellow bedtick has got all the realtors' wives by the ears. No civilized man ever seems to take part in its public life."

A decade after Mencken came Westbrook Pegler. "It is hereby earnestly proposed," he wrote, "that the U.S.A. would be much better off if that big, sprawling, incoherent, shapeless, slobbering civic idiot, the city of Los Angeles, could be declared incompetent and placed in charge of a guardian."

It is curious how the perceptions of Mencken and Pegler have persisted. In one of his plays, *California Suite*, Neil Simon had a New York visitor remark of our city that it "smells like an overripe cantaloupe." And more recently the Chicago columnist Mike Royko wrote that the entire state of California should be fenced in to protect the rest of the nation from its lunatics.

We have inspired dozens of memorable epithets, the most durable, perhaps, being Double Dubuque. That too goes back half a century. We have also been called the Nowhere City, Forty Suburbs in Search of a City, Smogville, the Fake Tomato Factory, and Cuckooland—the affectionate contribution of Will Rogers. Mencken himself summed us up in a word— Moronia.

Numerous of our critics have strangely hit upon the notion that Los Angeles lacks a sense of humor. Now that does pique me. I am not defensive. I don't wish to do anything to discourage this entertaining stream of invective. One of the delightful things about Los Angeles is that we inspire abuse. But it is axiomatic that a man can suffer almost any insult easier than the accusation that he lacks a sense of humor.

How can anyone say we have no sense of humor when we gave the world Sam Yorty, who thought he ought to be Secretary of Defense? And Ed Davis, who thought he ought to be governor? And Jerry Brown—who *is* governor? (And we all know what he thinks he *ought* to be.) You can't produce and enjoy leaders like those if you lack a sense of humor.

How can anyone say we have no sense of humor when we plant seventy-six thousand dollars' worth of plastic trees and flowers along one of our boulevards because otherwise, as one of our supervisors explained, "it would have been barren"?

What other city in the country has such a sense of humor that it could laugh at the construction of a million-dollar three-legged jukebox that was to be the very symbol of the city but which turned out to be sickly and was rendered silent, for the first several months of its life, by laryngitis? And what about our Diamond Lane? I can't recall any public folly that inspired more jokes, many of them very funny, than this wonderful notion that the way to ease traffic on the freeway during the rush hour was to close off one lane.

Being a newspaperman myself, I think I understand this evidently irresistible urge that Eastern journalists have to throw another cliché at Los Angeles. They are sent out here on expense accounts to write stories that will please their editors, and their editors want to be told that Los Angeles is a dreadful place, so they will feel better about living in New York or Boston or Philadelphia, especially in February.

The reporter settles into the Beverly Hills Hotel in an ambiance of cantaloupe and is taken out to Malibu on his first night to a freestyle moonlight party where he is intoxicated by palatable California wines and surprisingly literate and friendly natives, including relays of suntanned beach girls. The next morning he wakes up in his hotel room with his New England conscience and a hangover and feels guilty for having had such a wonderful time. He looks out his window and can't see the Empire State Building and is homesick. He calls room service and orders a bloody mary to exorcise his anomie, and while waiting for it he opens his portable typewriter and pecks out a few hundred words to reassure the folks back home that Nathanael West was right—that their correspondent is in the capital of kitsch at this very moment, wasting his talent away among Rotarians and retired chiropractors and mindless TV actresses in a plastic wasteland.

Somehow, though, I have survived this bleak environment and loved it, along with a few million others. Perhaps those of us who survive have survived for the same reasons. We have discovered that the real Los Angeles is invisible. It cannot be seen by visitors who hole up in the Polo Lounge or the Bistro or the steam room at the Beverly Hilton.

The real Los Angeles cannot be seen because it is to be found only in such invisible qualities as newness, openness, freedom, variety, tolerance, and optimism, and of course the weather—which is visible only when it's bad.

And no great harm is done, it seems to me, if we also have palm trees and suntanned beach girls. Nor by the fact that all of us are somewhat sunstruck, and we laugh a lot.

This book is not a tourist guide. It is not meant to be definitive. It is simply a glimpse into that invisible Los Angeles, which is real.

Jack Smith's

L.A.

1

Printers Ink

MATT WEINSTOCK

"He had his teeth in the leg of the bureaucratic beast."

Matt Weinstock died the other night of cancer.

We are moved, when a good man dies, to say that he cannot be replaced. It is a well-meant sentiment, and it is often believed, for a time.

Of Matt Weinstock, it happens to be true.

Men as honest and skilled and knowing will come along, surely. But they cannot replace him, because the place he held has gone with him.

Matt Weinstock *was* Los Angeles in a sense that no other man has been. He lived in and observed and wrote about a Los Angeles that existed only through him.

He was in touch, as it is no longer possible for a man to be, with the people of Los Angeles as individual human beings. He worked in his small office alone with his desk and his typewriter and his row of books, and he knew everybody.

Over the decades, as the metropolis grew bigger and stranger, and mere people seemed to melt into the concrete and the asphalt, they lived on in Matt Weinstock's daily column.

Hundreds of thousands of nobody people, who could not find their likenesses in the newspapers or on television or in the other mass outpourings of the modern media, read Matt Weinstock and knew they were still alive.

He was more than a person. He was a place—a meeting place, a part of Los Angeles, where those who were bruised, baffled or merely ignored could find grace.

No drunk fell so low that he might not find himself elevated in one of Matt Weinstock's anecdotes, the words as hard and shining and perfectly matched as a handful of dimes.

No housewife felt herself so abused, so frustrated, so put upon by the suburban rat race that she might not be restored to dignity and style, or at least good humor, by one short paragraph.

Nobody got into Matt Weinstock's column who didn't come out of it with class, including his perennial antagonist, El Jefe. Even the bad guys were somehow redeemed. He made them human, at least.

He was gentle, but he never gave up dogging the forces of oppression and obfuscation. He had his teeth in the leg of the bureaucratic beast, and every time he bit, it hollered.

He was as straight and astringent in speech as in prose. He was not given to profanity. But he knew there were bastards all about us, and he knew there was nothing else to call the bastards.

He had a decency in dealing with other people that seemed almost anachronistic. Reporters who knew him said he was always that way, as far back as they could remember.

More than thirty years ago a boy just out of high school, who had maybe seen *The Front Page* one time too many, walked brashly into the wonderful city room of the old *Daily News* to ask for a job.

Incredibly, the managing editor took him into his private office and talked to him, man to man, about newspapering. It was the Depression. There weren't any jobs. "But if you need work, for the time being," he told the awed boy, "maybe I can help you." Two days later he got the boy a job with a furniture company, moving furniture.

The managing editor was Matt Weinstock. I know, because I was the boy who got the job moving furniture.

It's a story Matt would have told better.

NICK WILLIAMS

"He is extremely effective with women, and vice versa."

Nick Williams retires this week as editor of the *Times* after forty years on this newspaper. For the past eighteen of those forty years Mr. Williams was my boss, though perhaps he never thought of his job in that way, having so many other problems.

There was a story in the paper the other day announcing his retirement and summarizing his career. It said things about Mr. Williams that I didn't know, and it left out some things I do know. In reminiscing about Mr. Williams I may seem to be talking more about myself than about him, but that is one of my weaknesses as a journalist, and one that Mr. Williams himself is well aware of.

A year or two ago when some columns I had done for the *Times* were to be published in book form, Mr. Williams agreeably consented to write a preface, and in it he said of me: "In a rather nice way he is a self-centered man."

Like everything else I ever saw that Mr. Williams wrote, that preface was brief, perceptive, and charming in its blunt felicity. As one reviewer said, "Even if you don't read the book, be sure to read the preface."

Perhaps I should point out that it's our style on the *Times* to call a man "Mr." only after he is dead, a requirement that Mr. Williams happily does not fill. However, Mr. Williams has always called me Mr. Smith and I have always called him Mr. Williams, and I am unable now to dismiss him simply as "Williams" because he is no longer editor.

One thing the story in the paper didn't say is that Mr. Williams is extremely effective with women, and vice versa. It often surprises lesser editors of the *Times'* editorial staff to discover that their wives have a crush on Mr. Williams and want to kiss him on his forehead, which has grown more spacious with the years.

The other side of that coin is that Mr. Williams, while he may stubbornly resist the advertising department, the circulation department, the publisher and if need be the President of the United States, can be melted by a single letter or phone call from a woman, especially if she is in tears or the least bit romantic. In a rather nice way he is a male chauvinist.

Some years ago when the column I was writing for the *Times* used to appear in a paper in Gary, Indiana, a girl who lived downstate in a little Indiana farm center wrote me a letter, thinking I was on the Gary paper, and invited me to her wedding. By chance I met Mr. Williams in the elevator that day and told him about the invitation, thinking it amusing.

"When a gentleman from the *Times* is invited to a young lady's wedding," said Mr. Williams, "he goes."

I went.

More recently, when my own son was to be married in France, I wrote that my wife would be going to the wedding, but I would have to stay home. A day or two later Mr. Williams called me to his office.

"What the hell are you trying to do to me?" he said, or something to that effect. "Women keep calling me up, wanting to know what kind of a man I am, not letting Jack Smith go to his own son's wedding."

I went.

Perhaps two or three times a year I received a memo from Mr. Williams. I have saved them. They are gems of brevity, clarity and wit, written with a soft copy pencil in Mr. Williams's scratchy hand on smudged little squares of paper, two or three short sentences at the most. Mr. Williams used his memos like rivets to hold us all together.

One of his memos was related to the preface he had written for me, in which he had said, "I don't think he will like me saying all this." When the galley proofs came I was dismayed to find that the book publishers had changed Mr. Williams's *me* to *my*, making it read, "I don't think he will like my saying all this."

I fired a letter off to New York, advising the publisher that Mr. Williams was known and envied throughout his profession for the vigor, grace and tone of his prose, a prose that often reflected his disdain for schoolbook grammar, and that their *my* was to be changed back to his *me*. But then I began to wonder if perhaps I should have consulted Mr. Williams first. I sent him a copy of the letter and asked him, "Did I do right?"

His answer came by memo in the interoffice mail: "You done superb."

The story in the paper didn't say that Mr. Williams grows roses; that he has the most astonishing private collection of starkly female nudes in La Canada, perhaps in the world; that he is the despair of prudes, phonies and tailors; nor that he has the most incisive and sophisticated mind of any person I know and is certainly one of the half dozen greatest metropolitan newspaper editors this country has ever had.

I don't think Mr. Williams will like me saying all this. But I am absolutely confident he will not change a word. He never has.

2
The More Things Change

THE ALEXANDRIA HOTEL

"Rudolph Valentino brought me on the streetcar . . ."

"Winston Churchill stayed here," the guide said, "and Sarah Bernhardt."

She was showing us through the old Alexandria Hotel, at Fifth and Spring streets. It had just reopened after its restoration to the Edwardian elegance of its heyday.

Winnie and the divine Sarah! I wondered if she meant they had stayed here together. It seemed unlikely. They were much too headstrong for each other, and it wouldn't have been good form.

She led us down a newly painted hall over a rich carpet to a corner suite.

"President William Howard Taft stayed here," she said, "and Woodrow Wilson."

I looked into the bathroom at the tub. It certainly wouldn't have done for Taft.

"In this very room?" I asked.

"We're not really sure."

The last time I had been in the Alexandria, it was a seedy has-been on the edge of exhaustion and oblivion. It was occupied then by the prizefight crowd and their hangers-on.

The grand ballroom on the second floor, where Mae Murray once twirled madly, had been made into a training gym. There was a roped ring at one end, in which two huffing brutes pawed hopelessly at each other in the smoky glare.

The lobby had that nowhere look of old hotel lobbies all over America, as cheerless as a prison waiting room. Along with its many coats of paint the grand dining room had acquired the drab patina and stale aroma of a skid-row mission mess hall.

Many of the guests had been holed up in their rooms upstairs for decades, through a dozen changes of management and wallpaper, and gave no sign of coming down alive.

As things go in Los Angeles, the Alexandria was ready for the wreckers.

It was rescued by a man named S. Jon Kreedman, who not only had faith in downtown Los Angeles but also in the power of nostalgia and the abiding values of the age of gaslight and exuberance.

Even as the last mansions were being razed on Bunker Hill, he was laying in rich red carpets and rolltop desks and Victorian settees and hanging brass-framed period portraits on the new red flock walls.

I lunched on artichoke hearts and rare roast beef in the Palm Court dining room. The carpet was rich of hue and texture. The walls were walnut and gold brocade. The old rose mirrors had been restored. The linen was white.

A rainbow light, green and amber and rose, fell from the original stained-glass panels in the ceiling. For nearly thirty years these lovely panels had been dark, covered by black paint from the blackout days of World War II.

Maybe S. Jon Kreedman has reversed the trend. Maybe others will have the curiosity to scrape off some black paint and see what kind of light can be let in from a past that we have scorned or forgotten.

Where else in this raw land can we lunch under a Tiffany skylight and summon up remembrance of things past?

The day the heat spell eased up I walked over to Fifth and Spring for the opening of the Francis X. Bushman suite in the Alexandria Hotel.

An invitation had come on the Alexandria's ornate stationery: "As a special friend of the late Francis X. Bushman, you are cordially invited to a champagne reception. . . . Mrs. Bushman and I certainly hope you will be able to join us."

I found the suite on the twelfth floor just down the hall from the Billie Dove suite and across from the Clark Gable. The walls were red flock, the carpet a deep red shag, the lamps ruby red. Francis X. Bushman's pictures hung on every wall, the great chin elevated, biceps flexed, eyes glaring down at the revelry in his suite.

I was looking up at a large framed picture of the star in some resplendent period uniform, helmet in hand, when Mrs. Bushman came along with a glass of champagne for me.

"What movie is that from?" I asked her.

"Why, *Graustark*," she said. "He was in so many of those mythical kingdom things, you know. He played so many kings and princes. Always in uniform, dashing about, saving the girl."

Mrs. Bushman was petite and vivacious, with platinum hair and purple eyes. She wore a blue satin dress with vermilion flowers, and gorgeous gold earrings set with large blue stones.

"I was determined not to wear red," she said. "It was Bushman's favorite color."

I asked about the stones in her earrings.

"Lapis lazuli and turquoise. I'm sorry to have to report they weren't cheap. I love costume jewelry."

She said she had been an agent before she married Bushman, not an actress, and her name was Iva. "I-v-a . . . same as always. People look at me and think I made it up, like Zsa Zsa. It's my name. My grandmother gave it to me."

I found myself alone with Claire Windsor at the hors d'oeuvre table. Her hair was gold, her eyes the improbable blue of an Alpine lake in early Technicolor.

"I remember being at this hotel once," she said. "Rudy Valentino brought me. He brought me on the streetcar, and he walked me home. I lived out in the Westlake district. We were both extras then, making five dollars a day. He did have something. Something in his eyes when he looked at you."

I hadn't seen Betty Bronson since *Peter Pan*. Her face looked as pert and fey as ever under the rolled-up brim of a yellow straw hat.

"My father used to bring me here," she was telling Bob Reis, the manager, "to piano concerts. He had two reasons. He wanted to hear the concerts, and he wanted to keep an eye on the piano. He had probably loaned them the piano. He was in the piano business. Isn't it fun the things that stick in your mind for years and years?"

Being in the piano business, her father knew many musicians, like the Hammersteins and Friml and Stravinsky. "I remember Stravinsky," she said, "for just one thing. He had an electric eraser. I've always wanted an electric eraser. Haven't you?"

Reis wondered if Miss Bronson and her father ever had the pecan punch in the Alexandria. "Evidently it was the thing. But we can't find the recipe."

"We always had the chocolate ice cream," said Miss Bronson.

Mrs. Bushman was posing for pictures with an enormous plaster-of-Paris bust of Bushman. "I had it done," she said. "Paid a lot for it. It was to go in the Hollywood museum, which never happened."

She was reminded of her late husband's taste for pillows. "Bushman was crazy for pillows," she said. "He'd have pillows all over the house. We'd go to Bullock's and buy thirty-five pillows at a time. When he was in a parade he'd be sitting on a pillow. For a man who was supposed to be as hardy as he was, he must have had a soft derriere."

She had been very devoted to Bushman. "I followed him everywhere, almost. Once a friend said to me, 'What are you ever going to do if he goes?' It's been five years this October, you know, since he passed. I said, 'I'm going to get rid of these damn bangs.' I don't know what it was that bangs did for Eisenhower and Bushman."

After the reception I walked back over the ruby-red carpet through the corridor to the elevator. A DO NOT DISTURB card hung from the doorknob of the Billie Dove suite, under the picture of Miss Dove.

There was life in the old place yet.

THE SUNSET STRIP

*"Elite revelers scrambled to snatch up the
dazzling fakes."*

The night it was hot and windy we drove out to the Sunset Strip for a hamburger. The sun was still up, having switched over to daylight savings time. The wind had worked hard all day to blow the smog off. In the dusk the city had the look of an old daguerreotype.

We drove up Sunset Boulevard at as slow a speed as the stream of Jaguars, Porsches, Volkswagens and Cadillacs would tolerate, looking at the signs and marquees just beginning to come to life in the twilight.

The boulevard was much more interesting than it used to be in what is thought of as its heyday, when it was expensive and chic, instead of expensive and hip, and real movie stars wore real diamonds and tuxedos to Ciro's and the Mocambo; and Mickey Cohen, the bush-league Al Capone, ran a haberdashery down the street from Ciro's as a front.

Local historians will cherish many stories of that quaint era before nudity supplanted glamour as the *sine qua non* of stardom: tales of lovemaking under the tablecloths; of one-punch, two-star fistfights; the night a pair of imported torpedoes hid in the shrubs across the street and shotgunned Neddie Herbert as he emerged from Sherry's with his claque of yesmen, a Judas, no doubt, among them.

The best one, though, was the night that mischievous Jim Moran swept into Ciro's in the robes of an oil-rich Arabian sheik, "accidentally" spilled a bag of phony rubies, diamonds and emeralds on the dance floor, then sat back philosophically considering the nature of his fellow man as the elite revelers, men and women, scrambled to their knees to snatch up the dazzling fakes with their bare hands.

The boulevard had become a midway of "total" nudie joints, hole-in-the-wall porno showrooms, elegant massage parlors, hamburger patios, organic food stores, discotheques, hip haberdasheries and novelty bazaars reeking of incense and glowing with fluorescent posters celebrating sex, peace and ecology, not a bad way to go.

We had No. 13 hamburgers on Alfie's patio, swept by the warm wind and looking off through the eucalyptus trees across the world's most indefinable city, which was just then putting on its own fake jewels for the night.

A man and woman took a table near ours, the man in a blue-and-yellow-striped tank shirt, what we used to call an undershirt, and the woman a tall suntanned beauty in oversize sunglasses, long brown hair and extraordinarily good long legs somewhat more than fully revealed by the most economical of hotpants.

"I might try one of those tank shirts," I whispered.

"Why?"

We drifted up the street and entered one of those flower culture marts whose voluptuous scent, psychedelic walls and irreverent bumper stickers momentarily disguise their essential character. They were only old-fashioned gift shops whose proprietors would just as soon have sold *Home Sweet Home* samplers and authorized photographs of J. Edgar Hoover if they ever came back in style.

While I was looking about, wondering if there was anything in the place I could possibly use, my wife bought seven sandalwood candles, a pair of wooden earrings and an ecological bumper sticker that was saved from obscenity only by its *double entendre* and its noble purpose.

I thought of buying a large ecological poster of a leggy Nordic blonde standing nude in a limpid mountain stream, but it would have upset the decor of my study, which is French impressionist.

As we left the store a nubile girl walked down the sidewalk in tie-dye bellbottoms carrying a cat in a baby blanket.

As I say, I found the Strip more interesting than it had been in the good old days. I could relate to it, in my fashion. Anyway, it beat waiting out in front of the Mocambo in hopes of seeing Rita Hayworth and only seeing Buster Crabbe.

THE CONTINENTAL BAR & GRILLE

*"The one-eyed bartender was the terrible
swift sword himself."*

The Los Angeles Convention Center is big and new, and we honor the big and the new.

The figures are impressive: a forty-million-dollar structure on thirty-one acres with a main hall the size of three football fields and the capacity to feed eight thousand people at one sitting.

At this point there is no use mourning the neighborhood that was leveled to make room for this awesome meeting place. It was a low-grade neighborhood at best, if not a slum; a seamy community of cheap bars, moldy hotels, poolhalls, pawnshops and the old *Herald-Express*, where I labored in the early 1950s. I shed no tears for the passing of this blight, except the *Herald-Express*. But there was one institution among all these caves, one oasis, that might serve as an inspiration to the management of the new center.

The trouble with any new structure anywhere, and especially one so vast, is that it lacks character; there is no mystique. No ghost in the walls, no great moments or personalities with which it is identified. I doubt very much if the management of the new center is aware that it stands on the site of the old Continental Bar & Grille, a place so rich in story, charm and personality that in the hearts of many of us old habitués its spirit still lives.

The Continental stood at Pico and Georgia, half a block from the Georgia Street Police Station and just around the corner from the *Herald*, whose wits, anecdotists and *bon vivants* it nurtured, usually on the cuff.

It may have been the longest bar in town. It was by all odds the noisiest. Conversation was impossible at any level below a shout. It had ambiance, a quality much in vogue among the classier saloons. The Continental had more ambiance than a bar needs, composed of noise, the smell of sour beer and old stew, and the personalities of Big Peggy, the house hustler; lesser temptations like Bucktooth Betty and Hophead Mary; and above all the absolute autocrat of the Continental, benign but omnipotent, the Terrible Swift Sword himself, George the one-eyed bartender.

Like few citizens outside our profession, George Banker had an unfailing belief in freedom of the press—a reverence. Occasionally he would collect a dollar bill from one of us, if we were flush; but otherwise it was on the cuff, a cuff which, as it turned out, went all the way up one of George's arms and down the other.

It was a pleasure to watch George bounce a troublemaker.

He not only had a bad eye but also a bad leg. He looked like the elder Lon Chaney made up as a one-eyed gimp, and it was beautiful to see when he put his dish towel down, lifted the gate and limped around the bar toward the doomed offender, this blind eye hideously open, his face suffused with love. Like Frankenstein's monster, George had a gentleness that made his wrath the more godawful.

Big Peggy was said to be as formidable a technician in her vocation as George in his, and, like George, it was understood, she cherished the freedom of the press. One of my colleagues on the paper, a man who has since achieved a gratifying literary esteem, kept Big Peggy on a permanent cash retainer, an arrangement which, I am quite sure, was never consummated.

I myself was very fond of Peg, but made only one business transaction with her, when my moron dog Shaggy had a litter of eight mongrel puppies and I sold one to this benevolent lady, across the bar, on credit.

The main ingredient of the Continental's character, the glue that held it all together, was the stew. I don't know what kind it was. I only know it was permanent. We never saw anyone making it, but the great kettle was always two-thirds full, bubbling malevolently at the back end of the bar, its odor of onion, turnips and soup bone permeating the dim noisy cavern year in and year out. Though I never came down hungry enough to taste it, I know for a fact that the Continental's stew was the staff of life on Pico Street.

If the management of the new convention center would name one of their many meeting rooms the Continental, they would honor its heritage, and many of us would be obliged.

As for the name of the center itself, I have another excellent idea. In the days when I worked at the *Herex*, as we called it, and George Banker presided over the Continental, the city room of the paper was run by Agness Underwood, a tough, sentimental, smart, generous, combative, bright, fair and infallibly intuitive Irishwoman who was so good at her work that she had reached the top in a profession jealously dominated by men almost as absolutely as the U.S. Marine Corps.

Aggie ran her city room the way George ran his bar, and hand in hand they kept the peace on Pico Street.

Aggie Underwood's aura, though, spread far beyond the

street. She knew the middle names, character flaws, private phone numbers and records of every ranking cop, politician and hoodlum in town, as well as their mistresses' names and private numbers. She kept this information in her head, at all times available for judicious use, along with such data as the birthdates of the district attorney and the mop boy at the Continental and what kind of liquor or neckties they liked. Aggie Underwood, I can testify, never used her awesome memory except in the interests of the First Amendment or the *Herald-Express*, whichever came first.

Now the *Herald-Express* is gone. The Continental bar is gone. George Banker is gone. Aggie Underwood, happily, is still around and sharp as ever. Only the other day she phoned me a tip on a story. She can't quit.

If the new convention center is to take any sustenance at all from the character and traditions of the neighborhood, I propose that it be named the Agness Underwood Convention Center and that the main bar be named the George Banker Bar & Grille. They are honest and indigenous, those names, and they will stand and grow like oaks in their native soil.

In time we will call it simply Aggie's Place.

3
Only in L.A.

LIFE AT THE BALTIMORE

*"What kind of people would name an iguana
Heathcliffe?"*

The other morning when it was too hot to do anything
rational I walked across town to call on the Benders. I had
recently received a letter from a man named William Bender
saying how much he and his wife Maggi loved Los Angeles.
They thought it was fascinating and beautiful.

It's not an extremely uncommon sentiment; but something about it seemed unusual. For one thing, Bender said that
he was manager of the Baltimore Hotel and that he and his
wife lived in. The Baltimore is at Fifth and Los Angeles, on the
edge of Skid Row. For another, he said they kept an iguana
named Heathcliffe. That made me curious. What kind of people would name an iguana Heathcliffe?

The Baltimore was built in 1909, but I found it in good
repair. Its guests come mostly from the nearby bus terminals
—transients and tourists from all over. It stands across the
street from the older King Edward, whose name is all that
remains of its palmy days. (Teddy Roosevelt built it, and his
initials may still be seen in the marble over the desk.)

The Benders had an apartment on the sixth floor of the
Baltimore looking into the air well. They turned out to be
youngish and sociable. You might meet them at any suburban
cocktail party. They seem delighted with their life-style.

"Most of my life," said Bender, "I lived in small towns.
Pennsylvania, Vermont. I have more identity here than I ever
had in small towns. We know everybody, all our neighbors.

Like Frank, the hallelujah man; Smokey the Bear; and Porno Bill. He runs the bookstore.

"It's only twelve minutes to the ballpark. It's only twelve blocks to the Music Center. Wonderful. We saw *Promises, Promises* twice and *Man of La Mancha* four times. It's fantastic the things there are to see."

"If you only look," said Maggi. "Everybody's in a hurry to get across the street before the light changes. They look down. They never look up at anything. Like . . . what are those things?"

"Gargoyles?"

"Nobody sees the gargoyles."

Bender has degrees in music and English and taught school before coming to Southern California for summer work and getting into the hotel business. They met in a little-theater group in Burlington, Vermont. "We were both in *The Glass Menagerie.* Maggi played my mother."

Then they were married and came to the Baltimore to live. They like the neighborhood. "It's safer here than anywhere in town. The winos don't bother you. They ask for money; that's all. Call an ambulance, it's here in five minutes. Call the police, they're already here."

"Everyone in this hotel," said Maggi, "treats me like a queen."

I saw the iguana on the back of a couch under the window. He had elevated himself on his legs like a dinosaur and was looking at me. He was a bright iridescent green, somewhat more than three feet long, counting his tail, which was marked off in rings of green and brown.

"Isn't he beautiful?" said Maggi.

The iguana ran down off the couch and into the next room, where he stood in a pool of light from a heat lamp. "He sits all day under that lamp," said Bender. "Even when it's hot like today."

"It's his security blanket," Maggi said.

There was a fake rubber tree in a pot near the heat lamp. "Heathcliffe sleeps in the tree," said Bender. There was a leaf of lettuce in a dish on the carpet. The iguana darted his tongue at the lettuce. "He touches everything with his tongue," said Maggi, "to see what it is."

"He eats lettuce and bananas, and sometimes we give him a grape. It's funny—he won't eat any kind of lettuce but one —what kind is it?"

"Bronze lettuce. He won't eat any kind but bronze."

I wondered if the iguana responded to human warmth, showed any kind of affection, like a dog. "When he's hungry," Bender said, "he'll come over and chew my shoe, or nibble at my toe."

"Is he full-grown?"

"Oh, no. He's only a year and a half. He'll get to be seven feet long and quite massive. When he gets too big, we're going to give him to the zoo."

"He's very beautiful," said Maggi, looking fondly down at Heathcliffe.

I walked back through town in the heat, past the King Edward and Porno Bill's, the pawnshops and nudie movies and beer caves. I took Main Street part way and Spring Street part way and at every corner I let one green light go by and looked up for gargoyles.

DRIVING THE FREEWAYS

"Even if we realized it was fun we'd never admit it."

Psychologists and others who worry about our minds like to add up the time we spend on freeways as so many hours out of our lives. It's a statistic that invariably turns up in books and articles about urban and suburban living.

Thus a man who lives in Covina and drives every day to a job in downtown Los Angeles is told that he spends nearly one month of every year on the freeway, and that's "one month out of his life."

Of course it isn't a month out of his life at all, but a month spent doing one thing when he might rather be doing another. Any man would prefer to be at home in his recliner with a martini in his hand than racing over a freeway or, worse, creeping over one.

On the other hand, driving a comfortable car over the freeway can be more pleasant than some of the things most of us do with the rest of our day, but I can't remember that anyone has ever said so before.

We've been told over and over that driving a car just to get from one place to another is a form of mental hibernation, and so we're unable to perceive its rewards. Even if we realized it was fun we'd never admit it; we'd cover it up like some kind of abnormality.

It occurred to me the other night as we were driving up the San Diego Freeway on our way back to Los Angeles from Mexico that the only time most of us have for idle reflection is behind the wheel.

It's the only time we're free: free from the telephone, free from things we ought to be doing, free from any kind of interruption but the occasional necessity of a prudent steering or braking to avoid catastrophe.

As we sped along my mind turned from one thought to another as easily as I turned the radio dial. I listened to some soul music and some kind of rock and then caught a big band playing *Bewitched, Bothered and Bewildered* and wondered if today's young people will feel nostalgic someday about Grand Funk Railroad.

The freeway flies through San Diego, circling downtown almost high enough to meet the jets coming in below the tops of the skyline, and it occurred to me that San Diego at night from the freeway is the prettiest American city I have seen, including San Francisco. I don't know of any prettier city in the daytime, either, if it doesn't get any bigger.

From Oceanside to the San Onofre nuclear energy station I worked on the purpose of life. It's a question I may be very close to answering, because I know now what the answer isn't. I figured that out one day at the beach. There is no use searching for some purpose intended by the Creator, as if He had contrived life as a kind of Chinese puzzle and was sitting up there waiting for us to make the right moves. No, He left the purpose up to us. That's the game. Our purpose is to invent a purpose. I was close to it, I think, when we got to San Clemente, but that reminded me of Richard Nixon and threw me off.

San Clemente also reminded me that neon lights, like freeways, are often scorned as gaudy, but they are really very pretty and cheerful, especially when you come up to a small town after a long haul through the dark and there is suddenly all that color and that happy writing . . . BEER . . . FOOD . . . COCKTAILS . . . It seems odd to think of light as drab, but after you have seen a town lit up with neon, a town with nothing but white lights looks drab. Ask an old truck driver if he doesn't like neon lights.

When we got home I knew myself a little better. I had organized a few things in my mind, made some plans and discarded a myth or two. I'd had a few laughs, sudden unexpected laughs that made my wife wake up, wondering what I was laughing at, because I had come across something funny in my mind, something that otherwise would have stayed in its cubbyhole until it was cobwebbed over and lost forever.

Of course you have to be an experienced freeway driver, or you're too anxious about the possibilities of imminent disaster to engage in metaphysical reflection. It is then simply a matter of prayer and reflex action.

I'm sure, though, that if psychologists would make a study of it they'd find that people who drive the freeways a month or so out of every year are the richer for it and are better adjusted than people who live close in. Of course I'm only guessing. I live close in.

PLASTIC SPRING

"They have virtues, too . . . they won't engage
publicly in sex."

Now and then it begins to look as if Los Angeles has lost its gift for doing the preposterous. New civic ventures are carried out with good taste. Architecture takes a turn toward art. The voters reject a demagogue. A landmark is spared. A prophet is honored.

At times like these I have a feeling of uneasiness. We couldn't afford to lose our image entirely. A Los Angeles that no one could laugh at might lose its magnetism. What if we were suddenly as sensible as Toledo?

So I was reassured the other day when I saw a story in the

paper about the county planting seventy-six thousand dollars' worth of plastic trees and flowers along a mile or two of parkway on Jefferson Boulevard.

There was a picture of some of the plastic plants, evidently growing out of a bed of crushed rock in the middle of the divider. They looked real enough, and yet they didn't. There was a quality of fantasy about them, like trees in a painting by Rousseau. They looked plastic. But I wasn't sure whether they looked plastic because they *were* plastic, or because I *knew* they were plastic.

But it's easy enough, I thought, to criticize a tree in a newspaper photograph. To be fair I'd have to drive out and see the plastic trees in actual life.

It was the other day when we had the light rain. I'd just as soon have stayed home, but I thought a plastic tree might look its best on a rainy day.

The stretch of Jefferson Boulevard which is planted to plastic trees is just west of Culver City, running along beside the Hughes Airport toward Playa del Rey. The boulevard is broad and divided here, and its only tenants opposite the airport are half a dozen modern industrial buildings, neatly landscaped.

When I saw the first clump of plastic plants I found myself laughing. They looked so absurd, so obviously unreal, so perfect, in a way. And yet maybe the laughter wasn't entirely cynical. I felt an admiration for these brazen frauds that would dare to compete with what only God can make.

The trees are planted, if that word is appropriate, in occasional islands, or planter boxes, along the parkway. There are half a dozen plants and trees in each. It is a very orderly grouping, no one plant being exactly the height of another, so that each cluster has the look of an arrangement. It is this arranged look, I think, as much as the nature of the plants, that makes them so unmistakably artificial.

I drove on down the boulevard, past island after island of plastic trees, none looking recognizably different from the other. This phenomenon went on for more than a mile and a half, and it occurred to me how quickly it had all come into being.

I've noticed that whenever any public work is undertaken against the public sentiment, the job is done quickly. The digging up of a street may drag on for months, but if a row of old palm trees is to be cut down, the trucks roll up in the morning and—zap!—it is done before sunset. Perhaps the same law works inversely. Real trees must be cut down and plastic trees must be planted before anyone knows what's happening.

I parked and walked out to an island to examine the trees close up. They were plastic, no doubt, stiff and indestructible-looking. Their trunks were made of steel pipe. They looked better from a moving car, but the rain helped. They were clean and shiny.

I haven't made up my mind about the plastic trees. They're rather pretty, in an unnatural way, like the plastic plants in aquariums. They'll be talked about, surely. They may help restore our image as one lifeless movie set.

But they have virtues, too. The frost won't get them, or the gophers. They won't drop leaves. They won't exude any exotic odors. They won't convert our carbon dioxide into oxygen. They won't engage publicly in sex. Besides, as one of our supervisors explained, the divider was too shallow to support botanical roots, so it was practically sterile. "If we hadn't planted plastic," he pointed out, "it would have been barren."

Maybe we'll grow to love our plastic plants. And then some morning early the trucks will come and—zap!—they will be gone.

Maybe for once we should try to save something before it's too late. Philistines, unite! Save our plastic vegetation and keep Los Angeles kitsch!

EARTHQUAKE

"That's a funny question to ask in the middle of an earthquake."

Having survived several disasters, including the bombing of Pearl Harbor, I have developed a habit of checking my watch whenever anything that might be historic occurs.

Thus, I am able later to say something like "We saw the first plane at 8:03 A.M. I know because I checked my watch."

This not only gives verisimilitude to one's account of great events but also a picture of a man with presence of mind, checking his watch at the onset of what might turn out to be a memorable calamity.

Consequently, when the earthquake struck last Wednesday, even though it shook me out of a pleasant sleep, I was alert enough to check my watch. I sleep with my watch on because I like to know what time I dream a particular dream. The trouble is, though, that I can't tell what time it is without my glasses, and it's no good sleeping with your glasses on.

It's my practice to leave my glasses on the table beside the bed, at hand for any emergency. There is no emergency I can't face up to better with glasses. That particular morning, however, they were not there. I groped for them as the house shook.

"Do you know where I left my glasses?" I asked my wife. She had been awakened by the earthquake too and was sitting straight up in bed.

"That's a funny question to ask," she said, "in the middle of an earthquake."

Fortunately, we were tuned in to Lohman and Barkley. We always seem to be tuned in to Lohman and Barkley when disaster comes. Not that I blame *them*. We had them on during the big earthquake of February 9, two years ago. Perhaps because of that experience they handled this one with poise and a gallant levity.

They didn't seem to have the slightest idea what was happening until Lohman's wife phoned. She told Lohman that their parrot had got out of his cage during the earthquake and damaged the plaster. It was the only report of damage I had heard up to that point.

"I didn't know Lohman was married," my wife said.

As for the earthquake itself, I have experienced better ones. By the time I found my glasses it was over. But nevertheless I had appraised it, subconsciously, perhaps, on my personal Richter scale. It was a 4.7. A 4.7 earthquake is entertaining. It does no serious damage, but it reminds us that the Republican Party isn't running everything. Or the Democratic Party either, depending on who's in.

People from elsewhere sometimes wonder why we live here in Los Angeles, where we are subject to earthquakes. After every earthquake, in fact, some are so frightened that they move back to the cyclone and hurricane country.

Perhaps what people fear about earthquakes is their unpredictability. There are no pre-earthquake signs in the sky. Clouds mean nothing. Neither do changes in the barometer. Even our gurus, the squarest of them, like Dr. Richter, for example, are unable to say when the earthquake god will next make his presence known.

I rather like earthquakes, myself, because they point up the human faculty for worrying about the wrong things. The chances that any particular person will be hurt by an earthquake in Los Angeles are so remote that insurance companies could get rich by betting against them.

Still, they always cause some damage.

While I was worrying about the Lohmans' parrot, my wife had gone into the kitchen and come back with some bad news.

"Well," she said, "it got our spices."

"My god," I said, not knowing what she meant.

She led me to the service porch, where the damage had occurred. It indeed had got our spices. She had been keeping them in a small cupboard, stacked one upon the other, in defiance of the principles of potential energy. When the earthquake came, naturally her unstable structure collapsed, leaving a tumbled heap of dill weed, ginger, bay leaves, marjoram, cloves and caraway.

I was amazed to see that we had so many spices which never seemed to get into our food.

"Were you afraid at all," I asked her, "when you knew we were having an earthquake?"

"No more than you," she said like a true Angeleno.

An occasional earthquake, I agree with her, is a good thing. It reminds us that men are not wholly in charge of their affairs and that a woman ought to keep her spices safe.

4
Westlake Park

WHAT'S IN A NAME

"The white flag soon went up over City Hall."

Many New Yorkers, according to a recent story in the *Los Angeles Times,* have refused to accept the change in the name of Sixth Avenue to Avenue of the Americas, although the change was procured nearly thirty years ago by a group of merchants who thought it would give that deteriorating street some class.

To this day, the story said, cab drivers given an Avenue of the Americas address are likely to turn on their passengers with a surly "You mean Sixth Avenue, don't you, Mac?"

Los Angeles has not been so loyal to its old place names. Too often we have stood by in apathy and watched them plucked like flowers from our garden. Most of these changes occurred during one or the other of this century's periodic wars, among whose lesser depredations have been this arrogant trampling of indigenous old names.

Our one surviving downtown park, for example, was known simply as Sixth Street Park when the city first moved that way. Then it became Central Park, probably because New York City had one.

But like many other peaceful places across the land, Central Park was a victim of World War I. Its name was changed officially to Pershing Square in honor of General John J. Pershing, commander of the American Expeditionary Force, a man of strong will and character whose highest service to his nation was in saving the American Army from the French generals.

Lincoln Park, out on the east side of town, started out, simply and logically, as East Lake Park. I don't know exactly when and why the change was made. I might have liked East Lake better, I think, but who can quarrel with Lincoln?

On the west side, before the century's first war, we had a small green place called Sunset Park. They called it that because in those days there was nothing between the park and the Pacific but the undulating plain, and the sunsets were superb. It is now called Lafayette Park, its name having been changed in a gesture of wartime amity between America and France.

Lafayette is a pretty name, and its bearer was a gallant soldier, more admired by small American schoolboys, in my day at least, than any other foreigner. We were all awed by the full spelling out in our history books of that splendid moniker —Marie Joseph Paul Yves Roch Gilbert du Motier, Marquis de Lafayette.

It seems to me, though, that Lafayette's assistance in the Revolution would have been adequately repaid by the landing of the AEF in France, without giving him one of our parks, way out here in Los Angeles, like a posthumous medal on his breast.

Between wars, parks are fairly safe. Now and then, the record shows, a supervisor or a city councilman will grab one off, and they are never safe, of course, from mayors. But unfortunately we have more generals than parks.

The last to go was Westlake. It had been known as Westlake since the nineteenth century, this beautiful suburban oasis that grew up around a natural pond. Soon it was surrounded by Victorian homes and hotels. Birds and ducks flew in for sanctuary. Canoes and electric motorboats appeared on its placid waters, poking among the water lilies. Westlake was a haven, as peaceful as a painting.

Now it is MacArthur Park, and the general's statue still stands in the park above a dried-up pool. He looks rigid and abandoned, as if trying to escape his last Corregidor.

It seems that the people in the beginning give places names that are simple and vivid and appropriate. They spring from the soil. East Lake, Westlake. Sunset. Central. And then the ambitious or jingoistic little committees march in and do their banal work. Bureaucrats have a weakness for obliterating traditional and euphonious place names to immortalize some colleague or leader, especially one who has fallen and is no longer a threat.

Thus, Boulder Dam became Hoover Dam, Cape Canaveral became Cape Kennedy, and more recently and closer to home our Caltech Jet Propulsion Laboratory became the H. Allen Smith Laboratory, in honor of the former Republican representative from Glendale. Fortunately, sanity prevailed in the Canaveral and JPL affairs, and the old names were restored.

But unfortunately, Democrats in Congress lost their fight to change Hoover Dam back to Boulder Dam, despite an ingenious suggestion that the contest be resolved by changing the name of the thirty-first President of the United States to Herbert C. Boulder.

It was City Hall that changed Westlake Park to MacArthur Park back in World War II when Douglas MacArthur was island-hopping across the Pacific. As far as I know, General MacArthur had never laid eyes on Westlake Park, nor did he even drive a few blocks out of his way to take a look at it after the war when he made his celebrated old-soldier talk at the Ambassador Hotel.

I don't believe this story has ever been told in print, but Westlake Park was changed to MacArthur Park as the result of unrelenting pressure on City Hall by William Randolph Hearst, whose motive was the promotion of MacArthur for President. Hearst ordered his local newspaper to procure this MacArthurization of Westlake, and one of its toughest and sharpest political reporters was assigned full time to the job.

The white flag soon went up over City Hall, and the park not only got its new name, but there was a noisy parade down Wilshire Boulevard and a number of speeches in the park, none of which, I'm sure, mentioned the true author of the entire cynical farce.

Westlake is a rundown neighborhood today, but it still has a certain charm, perhaps nostalgic. Some of the city's best old Victorian houses surrounded the park, and the business district looks almost unchanged since the 1930s. The people who live in the neighborhood call it Westlake, and they trade at the Westlake Cleaners and the Westlake Outlet Store and go to the Westlake Theater. I don't remember anything in the neighborhood called MacArthur but the park itself.

I suppose there is no political reason for changing the name back to Westlake. On the other hand, I doubt if there is any political reason against it. The nation found its war hero in Dwight Eisenhower, and as Douglas MacArthur had predicted, he simply faded away. Actually, I always admired MacArthur as a soldier; I think he was almost as brilliant as he thought he was. But I imagine his place in history will not depend on whether a little park in Los Angeles bears his name or not.

My friend and colleague Matt Weinstock knew the real story, and he never sold out. He always called the park MacWestlake. But I won't even go that far.

The general is MacArthur; the park is Westlake, and I think the name should be restored.

To arms!

Now a man who played an inside role in the change of Westlake to MacArthur takes issue with my summary of the affair.

"I served as deputy mayor at the time," writes Frank Peterson. "One morning Carl Greenberg, political reporter for the *Examiner*, came to my office and informed me that William Randolph Hearst wanted Westlake Park changed to MacArthur Park and could I help him . . . his job was on the line. . . . I took Mr. Greenberg to Mayor Bowron's office; the mayor thought it was a great idea and that's all there was to it. There was no 'unrelenting pressure' as you state. Neither was there 'a noisy parade down Wilshire Boulevard. . . .' "

That sounds as if the mayor simply said "So be it" and it was done. The truth is that the machinations went on for weeks. In March the park commission voted the proposal down. Two months later, without a public hearing, they approved it. They had to hurry because June 13 was to be MacArthur Day, and the mayor wanted, as he put it, "a celebration the like of which has never been seen in Los Angeles. . . ."

A few days later, when the word reached Westlake Park, a large and angry group appeared at City Hall in protest. Their neighborhood had been stripped of its identity and without a hearing. They grew even angrier when the mayor disclosed that General MacArthur had already been notified by radio.

The day might have been won by the anti-MacArthurs but at that very moment the general's acceptance reached the mayor's desk by radiogram from SOMEWHERE IN THE SOUTH PACIFIC. The mayor read it aloud:

TO BE THUS HONORED BY THE CITIZENS OF YOUR GREAT CITY MOVES ME DEEPLY. THEIR ACTION CAN ONLY BE MOTIVATED BY A NOBLE IMPULSE TO COMMEMORATE THE IMPERISHABLE FEATS OF THE GALLANT SOLDIERS WHOM I HAVE COMMANDED. AS SUCH IT WILL STAND FOR ALL EYES FOR ALL TIME AS A SYMBOL OF THE INVINCIBLE DETERMINATION OF OUR BELOVED COUNTRY FOR VICTORY.

MACARTHUR

Awed by the general's orotund rhetoric, the crowd fell silent. It seemed nothing less than an act of divine intervention.

MacArthur Day went off as scheduled. The next day the *Times* reported as follows:

The parade which preceded the ceremony moved along Wilshire Boulevard from Union Avenue behind an Army color guard and band, and the Army's might was represented by infantrymen and men riding service trucks and armored cars. State guardsmen, veterans groups, Red Cross units and numerous bands made up the procession which poured into the park for almost an hour. A howitzer fired one round to open the program. A seventeen-gun salute to General MacArthur roared a closing finale, followed by the singing of the National Anthem by Risë Stevens.

Meaning no disrespect for Risë Stevens, I must say that sounds like a fairly noisy day.

If it hadn't rained, if Wellington's center hadn't held, if Blucher hadn't arrived in time, Napoleon might have won the battle of Waterloo, and history would have taken quite another road.

If I hadn't taken a trip to the frozen Middle West and come home with the flu and laryngitis, in no condition to lead the charge, we might have won our battle to restore the historic name of Westlake to MacArthur Park.

The crisis came at a public hearing before the Parks and

Recreation Commission. You may have read the story in the paper. Six citizens showed up, five of them in favor of Mac-Arthur. Reading this as a lack of public interest, the commission's president cast the deciding vote, and Westlake Park went down the drain, three to two, perhaps forever. It was one more victory for the hero of Luzon.

To those who had earlier rallied with such spirit to my vainglorious call, I apologize abjectly. In the clutch, unhorsed, I left them without a captain. Though my files bulge with letters from volunteers avowing loyalty to the cause, I didn't get back in time to publish a notice of the hearing, as I had hoped to do. Evidently the news had not reached my battalions by other means. They waited vainly for the bugle's sound.

Heavy of heart, I now dismiss them with my gratitude. Back to your plows. I am off to Elba. I would like to say, "I shall return." But I suppose the confidence of my troops is lost forever. History does not wait for those who are late at the crossroads.

All the same, I will always call it Westlake.

AETNA LIFE AND OTIS ART

"Suddenly a young woman threw off a robe and began posing in the nude."

Out near Westlake Park a gratifying kind of rapport has been achieved between the young students of the Otis Art Institute and an insurance company in the upper floors of a thirteen-story building across the street.

The tale came to me from Herb Allen, of Allen, Simonds, Gates & Company, insurance brokers, and I dropped in at his office the other morning to check it out at the scene.

The art institute and the American Cement Building stand facing each other on Wilshire Boulevard, just west of the park. The top six floors of the taller building are occupied by the Aetna Life & Casualty Insurance Company, which in turn subleases some of its space to other firms, such as Allen's.

His offices are on the thirteenth floor, looking down not

only on the park, which appears serene and beautiful from that height, but also on the roof of the Otis Art Institute. It was this chance perspective that eventually brought students and businessmen together.

"For eleven years," Allen said as we looked down at the institute from his window, "there's been a peaceful coexistence between Aetna and Otis. But generally Aetna represents one world and Otis another."

Aetna's offices are all glass on the Wilshire side, however, and it was inevitable that the men of the insurance firm would sometimes look down into the institute's courtyard, perhaps wistfully.

"The girls wear long hair and tight pants and no makeup and no bras," Allen said. "Sometimes they play volleyball there in the courtyard and on May Day they dance around the Maypole. We've always kind of watched what was going on."

Then one sunny afternoon about two months ago something new came into the picture. A sculpture class appeared suddenly on the roof of the institute and a young woman threw off a robe and began posing in the nude.

"Things ground to a halt at Aetna," Allen recalled. "The whole building tilted toward the institute, from employees rushing over to the windows. This went on for three-quarters of an hour."

Naturally, the male employees of Aetna were delighted. Naturally also, their manager, Walter White, Jr., was not. A nude model on a rooftop was a casualty Aetna was not set up to underwrite.

"Mr. White is a fine man and a good manager," Allen said, "but he thought Aetna might be better off if they helped the sculpture class to rent a studio and stay off the roof."

Though the insurance men kept a vigil after that, weeks went by and the sculpture class failed to appear on the roof again. At this point Allen had an inspiration. He walked over to the institute and made a few discreet contacts. A day or two later two students appeared on the roof with the model.

"The first time," Allen said, "she had been demure. This time she slipped out of her robe, faced the Cement Building and threw her shoulders back. It was a great performance."

The class was supposed to continue for ten or fifteen minutes, after which, according to Allen's plan, the two students were to unfurl a long banner with a message for the spectators across the street.

But something went wrong. Before the climax could take place, someone dashed out on the roof and remonstrated with the students. They put away their work and the model slipped into her robe and the three of them left the roof.

"It was a great disappointment," Allen recalled. "Evidently someone from Aetna had telephoned the dean. I was sure my plan had gone awry."

Then suddenly the model came back.

"She'd forgotten her little yellow umbrella. She saw the banner, and all by herself she rolled it out. I LOVE YOU WALTER WHITE, it said. It was lovely."

Since then, alas, the sculpture class has stayed below. But there's a volleyball game almost every day. May Day will soon be here. The girls at Aetna are beginning to look more like the girls at Otis. And everybody loves Walter White.

MARY CLARK

"One of the men started cussing me . . .
for feeding the birds."

There was a telephone message waiting for me in my office the other morning from Mary Clark of the Leighton Hotel. She had called twice. "Has something to tell you," the note said. Evidently it was urgent.

I called the Leighton, but Mary Clark could not be found. It was hot downtown, and I thought it wouldn't hurt me to drive out to the Leighton, find out what Miss Clark wanted and take a walk in Westlake Park.

The Leighton is on Sixth Street across the street from the park, a turn-of-the-century relic with cupolas and a courtyard. Before World War I there could have been no better address, but over the decades the Leighton declined with the neighborhood, and in recent years it has become a home for senior citizens.

There is a broad arched porch on which three elderly gentlemen sat, thoroughly engaged at the moment in watching me walk through the courtyard and up the steps. We all said hello.

The lobby still bore heavy traces of a lost opulence; overweight mahogany furniture, an enormous oil portrait in the manner of Gainsborough and huge mirrors in ornate gilded frames. It was dark and quiet. There was no one at the desk.

Two women sat in chairs against the opposite wall. Their conversation had stopped. I walked over and asked if they knew Mary Clark.

"Why, yes," said one. "Her room's right over there. Here, I'll show you."

Miss Clark lived in a room just off the lobby. She was in. I introduced myself. "You had something to tell me?"

"Why, bless you," she said. "Come in. I hope you'll excuse this room." She offered me a chair by the window, which opened onto the courtyard. "Will that be too windy for you?"

"I don't think so," I said.

Mary Clark sat on the edge of her bed, which was covered by a cheerful red spread. The room had a pleasant clutter of envelopes and greeting cards and the little totems that people collect to remember by.

"Well, Miss Clark," I said, "what's on your mind?"

"Yes. Well, you know I feed the birds, over in the park. Oh, yes. I lived here when I was a girl. We moved to a house on Bonnie Brae in 1902. I was fourteen years old. We used to swim in the little lake. It was clear as crystal then. And we used to feed the birds. Oh, there were thousands of birds."

In time she had married and moved away, and then four years ago, at eighty, she had come back, to live at the Leighton. The story she wanted to tell me was about a man, another resident of the Leighton, who had given her a hundred dollars to buy food for the birds. He had promised her one Sunday that he was going to do it, and the next morning it happened.

"I was right across the street there, feeding the birds. There was a line of people on the sidewalk waiting for a bus, and one of the men started cussing me."

"Cussing you?"

"For feeding the birds. And then this man came running

across the street to catch the bus and he said, 'Oh, here's your money,' and he reached in his pocket and gave me this hundred-dollar check."

"That's remarkable," I said.

"Do you want to know the man's name?"

"Yes," I said, "I think I ought to."

"Just a minute. I've got it right here." She picked up a little note pad and searched it up and down through a magnifying glass. "Here it is. R-o-b . . . Oh, Robert . . . G-e-t-c-h-e-l. Getchel. Robert Getchel."

I wrote it down.

"What do you think, Miss Clark," I asked, "about their changing the name of the park from Westlake to MacArthur?"

"Well, what did you think when they changed the name of that little park downtown to Pershing Square?"

Mary Clark was one war ahead of me.

5

The Passing Scene

DOWNTOWN

*"We're hoping that all the excitement will bring back
the pretty girls. . . ."*

The banks are playing a game of skyscraper chess downtown, and United California Bank has made the latest move.

I realized this with a jolt a week or two ago when I was having lunch in the Mistele at the top of the forty-two-story Crocker Tower. I had taken a friend up to show her the view, which not too long ago was unobstructed.

This time, though, there was a startling intrusion in the picture. A dark vertical bar now stood to the west, blacking out the Wilshire corridor, Beverly Hills and Century City like a strip of censor's tape.

It was United California Bank's new headquarters building at Sixth and Hope, a block west of the Crocker Tower. It loomed twenty stories above us—sixty-two stories high and the new king of the downtown skyline.

It was UCB that had made the first move, not very many years ago, when it put up a sixteen-story building at Sixth and Spring in the heart of the old financial district. It was the city's first building, except City Hall, to break the earthquake limit of thirteen stories.

Then came Occidental Center with its tower rising thirty-two stories at Eleventh and Hill. For a time the Occidental Tower stood in isolation above the stubby city, like some splendid error. Then the money began to move west on Sixth Street to the neighborhood of the library and Pershing Square, and the game was on in earnest.

Union Bank built sixty-four feet higher than Occidental.

Then Crocker went up eighty-six feet higher than UB. Then Atlantic Richfield and Bank of America put up twins, each ninety-seven feet above the Crocker.

I remembered the exhilaration of my first ride to the top of the Arco Tower, from which the view, as it had once been from the Crocker, was unblemished by competitors. Those were heady days for Arco and the Bank of America, though not without their embarrassing moments, one being the discovery that when the bank's directors assembled in their board room to contemplate their empire they looked straight out to a white tower on their east with fourteen-foot-high letters saying CROCKER BANK.

Now United California Bank had played its king, and it stood one hundred and fifty-six feet above the twins. Live by the sword, die by the sword.

The magnetism moves to the new champion. I wondered what the world might look like from the top of the UCB. Last Tuesday, in the company of two gentlemen from the bank, I found out. It looked wet.

It was the day the "unexpected" storm came, blowing in from the ocean. The three of us rode up to the top of the building in the work elevator. The windows were already in on the lower stories, but the top was open and windswept. Rain had made a muck of the floor. We approached the yawning edges with care. Below us, the great Los Angeles plain was under wraps.

"Lousy day," said one of the others. "Reminds me of Boston in the fall."

One block up Hope, to the north, the old library seemed more antique than ever. Beyond it a new steel tower was growing on Bunker Hill. In the near distance the Music Center had a soft gleam in the opaque sky, recalling my first sight of the Parthenon, bone-colored in a storm over Athens.

We looked down on the roofs of the lesser towers, from which steam billowed up to join the clouds. We could see desks and people through the hundreds of amber windows. In the fall, they said, this building would be joining that new downtown life system.

It was raining hard when we reached the sidewalk again. People huddled in storefronts, waiting it out. No one is ever dressed for a storm in Los Angeles. A pretty girl in a minidress stood in front of the Crocker Bank. She held a plastic umbrella through which the light fell softly on blond hair. Her legs were sheathed in nylon, and faultless.

"Ah, yes," said one of the UCB men as we admired her from across the street. "We're hoping that all the excitement down here, this new life, will bring back the pretty girls. They've all gone out to Beverly Hills and Century City."

Perhaps the ecologists will keep that in mind when they ponder the impact of the skyscraper on downtown life. Pretty girls are part of the system, too.

WORLD'S GREATEST CITY

*"Los Angeles has become . . . a longing
in men's breasts."*

Hollywood's moviemakers have always been called the great American dream merchants, not without a touch of irony. But the real dream merchants weren't out in Hollywood. They were downtown.

The real dream merchants of Los Angeles didn't sell movies; they sold Los Angeles; and somewhere between the fantasies of the city builders, the reality of Los Angeles was lost, never to be found.

It was in the effervescent 1920s that we sang our siren song the loudest. A reader, Walter Kempthorne, has sent me an elaborate brochure published in 1923 by a downtown Los Angeles investment firm. It is typical of the time and modestly entitled "Why Los Angeles Will Become the World's Greatest City."

At the heart of this thesis was a drawing by Charles H. Owens, the skillful artist of the *Times*, envisioning a magnificent parkway winding through "a Valley of Golden Apples" from Westlake Park to the sea at Santa Monica.

"A glorious ribbon of parks, arches, monuments, fountains and public edifices," read the florescent text, "a valley delectable with a balm of orange blossoms and profusion of flowers . . . through foothills rivaling Athens and Monaco combined. . . ."

Along this magnificent route, the enchanted traveler would come upon such public ornaments as the Fountain of Progress, the Fountain of the Western Spirit, a great convention center, a monumental domed Hall to the U.S. Presidents (just west of the Los Angeles Country Club), a Fountain of Youth, a Fountain of the Winds, a dozen memorial arches, and at the seashore an enormous California Arch, beyond which the great boulevard ran out into the shining bay to end in a grand pavilion.

It was not a vision that sprang only from the mind of the artist. It was a serious project, conceived and endorsed by responsible civic men and institutions. This super ribbon was to unwind not only westward to the Pacific, but eastward to the "Rim of the World" in the San Bernardino Mountains. It would be, the brochure promised, nothing less than "the finest boulevard of the New World."

"Los Angeles," the brochure said, "has touched the imagination of America. She has become an idea . . . a longing in men's breasts. She is the symbol of a new civilization, a new hope, another try. . . ."

It was God's own spa. It was the place of the perfect society at last, where all classes prospered and all men were equal under the sun, though one might live in a great house and drive a Pierce-Arrow and another live in a cottage and drive a flivver.

"The time is almost here when Southern California, with Los Angeles at the center, will be studded and gemmed with the most beautiful homes of America, or of the modern world, all set in an embroidery of parks and gardens . . . and in these parks and gardens, adjacent to the homes of grandeur, will snuggle the exquisite little homes of the middle-class man, the reality of his dreams."

In footnotes, the brochure offered testimonials of celebrated contemporaries such as Marshal Foch, the hero of France, who was quoted as saying, "If I had to start life over again I would go to Los Angeles."

In the end, the poet of the brochure recognized the affinity between the dreams he spun and the dreams of Hollywood.

"The visual truth of our printed words has gone forth over

this country and Europe in the photoplays ... creating the psychological impression in the minds of millions that it is the place where dreams come true, the veritable Land of Heart's Desire. ... Can there be any doubt but that Los Angeles is to be the world's greatest city ... greatest in all the annals of history?"

The truth is, they did get started with it. They built an Egyptian temple downtown for a library, and they built a Byzantine university in the hills near the western end of their dream street, not knowing that those annals of history held in store a great Depression and three wars.

Oh, well. As the brochure said, it's the place of another try.

BRITANNICA'S L.A.

"You must tell people they don't have much time."

The Encyclopædia Britannica is not what you would call a trendy publication. It is coming out next month with the first new edition since the fourteenth edition was published in 1929.

The new edition of EB will have exactly 6,760 words on Los Angeles. I can vouch for the accuracy of that figure because the Los Angeles entry was written by a friend of mine, John D. Weaver, and he had his wife Harriett count the words.

The article is a triumph of condensation, so loaded with facts that it ought to sink of its own weight, but it is buoyed up by Weaver's style, insights and asides.

In the first paragraph he sets the scene like a novelist: "A semitropical Southern California metropolis of palm trees and oil derricks, television studios and aerospace factories, Los Angeles is the third largest city in the United States. ... It has paid for its spectacular growth by acquiring such contemporary urban attributes as smog-drenched skies, a polluted harbor, clogged freeways, explosive ghettos, overcrowded schools and annual budgets teetering on the brink of bankruptcy. ...

"Its hallmark is a 620-mile-long network of freeways that

provide moving parking places for the county's four million cars and trucks. Angelenos commute, shop, bank and breed by automobile. [He might have added worship.] The vehicle so dominates the life of this uniquely mobile community that a visiting English architectural critic, taking his cue from intellectuals who study Italian in order to read Dante, is said to have learned to drive a car so he could 'read Los Angeles in the original.' "

Tracing our history, he takes us from the Indian village of Yang-na to the contemporary city "grotesquely shaped, like a charred scrap of paper. . . ." He notes that Hollywood was laid out in 1887 by Horace Wilcox, "a Prohibitionist who intended his subdivision to be a sober, God-fearing community," and that a one-mile section of Sunset Boulevard known as The Strip is "one of the few places where Angelenos stroll and take the sun at sidewalk cafes."

Under the subheading "Climate," he observes: "Nothing is predictable in this unpredictable land, least of all the weather, which is usually described as unusual."

He quotes Raymond Chandler on the psychological perils of our Santa Ana winds ("Meek little wives feel the edge of the carving knife and study their husbands' necks") and again on the pensioners who once lived in seedy Gothic mansions on Bunker Hill. ("On the wide cool front porches, reaching their cracked shoes into the sun, and staring at nothing, sit the old men with faces like lost battles.")

And today, he observes, "brisk successful lawyers, stockbrokers, and government officials live in skyscraper apartments on the leveled hill, within walking distance of the county courthouse, the bourse, and a massive civic centre. . . ."

In forty-eight words, he says more about the Watts Towers than most of us know: "The three Watts Towers (99, 97, and 55 feet high) in the Watts section were built of broken tiles, dishes, bottles and seashells over a 33-year period by Simon Rodia, an unschooled Italian immigrant who later explained, 'I had in mind to do something big, and I did.' "

He does not slight our crucial problems, and at the end he quotes a warning given by the late Aldous Huxley a decade ago: "You must tell people they don't have much time."

It happens that among my treasures is the ninth edition of

the *Encyclopædia Britannica,* published in 1892. In that edition, I find, Los Angeles was given exactly 197 words, of which perhaps the most significant are these: "As the centre of a fine orange and grape growing country, and a resort for invalids, Los Angeles is a place of some importance."

In the judgment of EB's editors back in 1892, though, we were not nearly as important as the lory, which was the subject of the article immediately preceding the one on Los Angeles. The lory received 674 words, or exactly 477 more than Los Angeles.

A lory, if you didn't know, is a species of richly colored parrot found in the jungles of New Guinea.

THE CANNON

"They came in the night . . . and stole it away."

I was driving out Monterey Road in San Marino the other morning and noticed that the old cannon was missing from the lawn in front of the Southwestern Academy.

It had stood there as long as I could remember, a memento of some war long lost. As a landmark it made no sense on that sylvan street. But we are short on historical landmarks; too often they are done away with in the night.

I parked and walked over the lawn to the place where the cannon had stood. There was a broken concrete foundation and two rusted stubs of steel cable. The gun evidently had been torn loose and hauled away. That would have been no easy task.

I found Kenneth Veronda, director of the academy, alone in his office, a young man wearing a red sweater with the academy's emblem. I came right to the point. "What has become of the cannon?"

"Ah, yes," he said. "The cannon. They came in the night, one moonlit night, and stole it away."

"Who stole it away?"

"The students from Caltech."

It had been in the papers at the time, but I had missed it. Anyway, I had a special interest. Veronda had written me, a year or so earlier, after I had called Monterey Road one of the most beautiful residential streets in Southern California. He had been pleased but had apologized for the cannon, saying it fit neither the peaceful atmosphere of the neighborhood nor the image of the academy, which was not in any sense a military school.

The cannon was, in fact, an embarrassment, a white elephant. But it was a family heirloom, so to speak, and hard to get rid of.

"Where did it come from?" I asked.

The French had made the gun in 1871 for the Franco-Prussian war, but too late; it never fired a shot. In 1896 the U.S. Government took it on loan and rifled the barrel for the Spanish-American War; again it never fired a shot. In 1904 the French hoped to sell it for the Russo-Japanese War, but Teddy Roosevelt quickly got that war stopped.

"Finally," said Veronda, "they sent it out to Santa Barbara, where it was placed on the lawn in front of the French consul general's summer home, and he was stuck with it."

In 1924, though, Veronda's father founded the Southwestern Academy. The current French consul general saw this as a splendid opportunity. He sent the cannon to the elder Veronda as a gift of state. The academy had been stuck with it ever since—until that recent moonlit night.

"I was watching from the tower," recalled Veronda, making a tacit admission of collusion. The operation was staged by Fleming House, a Caltech campus residence. There were seventy or eighty in the party, including girls. "They worked in utter silence. Orders were given by hand signal."

The gun was cut loose. Planks were laid out across the lawn. Then the entire Fleming house contingent shouldered the ropes and dragged the cannon into the street.

"The barrel is twelve feet long, and the students said later the gun weighed one and seven-tenths tons. They moved it by hand, all the way. Three miles over Oak Knoll from here to Caltech. It was two o'clock in the morning. And all you could hear was the shuffling of feet."

I drove over to Caltech to see the cannon in its new location. It stood directly in front of Fleming House, in dead center of Olive Walk, Caltech's cherished main street.

I had forgotten how big the gun was. It seemed too big for

those foolish little wars. Its wheels were five feet high and its barrel was over my head. It was aimed down Olive Walk, point-blank at the classic façade of the Faculty Club.

I thought it looked a bit ridiculous. It seemed as out of place here as it had in front of the academy.

But you have to like a cannon that has had the sense to miss action in three of history's silliest wars, spend fifty years at a peaceful boys' school and finally make it into Caltech.

CATALINA ISLAND

*"The pilot cranked the wheels down and
we crawled up the ramp."*

The summer season being over, I drove down to San Pedro the other morning and caught a seaplane over to Catalina. All places, to my mind, are better out of season.

My idea of travel would be to wander over the earth without plan, making sure only that I arrived at every new place a week or two after its season had ended, when the local people had settled back into their out-of-season pace and the weather had turned sullen and perverse.

A few years ago my wife and I were in southern Italy in the winter. We walked over the stones of Pompeii in the rain and when we reached Sorrento there was thunder and lightning all night long. The next morning the Bay of Naples was too rough for the excursion boat and we couldn't go to Capri. Too bad; I would like to have seen Capri in a storm.

There was an open seat on the 10:30 flight to Avalon, and less than five minutes after I reached the terminal I was in place at the rear of one of Air Catalina's quaint old amphibians. The pilot looked familiar. He had a weathered face and a gray walrus mustache and wore an old sweater and jeans and a white canvas sailor's hat with the brim turned down all around, like a little boy at the beach. I had flown with him before.

A ground-crew man with long hair stuck his head in the plane and said, "Fasten your seat belts, no smoking in flight."

He slammed the door shut and at once we waddled down the ramp into the water. This is the most casual and safest of airlines.

The pilot cranked the wheels up with his hand crank and gunned the motors. White spray blew by the windows as we planed over the channel and took off. Fifteen minutes later we landed off Pebbly Beach with a marvelous splash. The pilot cranked the wheels down and we crawled up the ramp.

In Avalon Bay the excursion boat had just arrived from San Pedro, and a hundred visitors or so were strolling along the wharf toward the town. They were soon scattered along Crescent Avenue, enough people to give a sense of life, but not a crowd. The mainland had been overcast; Avalon was in the sun.

There were subtle changes, but they were hard to see. Avalon still looked incredibly like the picture postcards of the 1930s. It had changed less, surely, than any other Southern California town. The landmarks were all in their places: the old Zane Grey house, the Glenmore, the Catalina, the Wrigley mansion, the Casino, the Tuna Club. Except for a few coats of paint, I would have guessed, the Tuna Club hadn't changed since Herbert Hoover became a member.

I walked half a block up from the bay to the City Hall to call on Ray Rydell, the mayor. He was out on the sidewalk, a suntanned man in a black-and-white check shirt, tan shorts and tennis shoes. He looked more like Bobby Riggs than the mayor of a city.

We walked down to the Bay. Avalon, the mayor said, was changing, and it would change more; but very gradually, and that was the way he wanted it. A condominium was coming, but so far no high-rise. Avalon wanted to grow, but not to explode. "It's a very hard thing to do," he said.

Already there were a thousand automobiles on the island. But at its last meeting the city council had passed a law under which no vehicle could be brought in without a permit granted by a five-man board. I hoped it wasn't too late.

Rydell had been drawn back to the island by nostalgia. "This was always my second home. I learned to swim right here in this bay. I used to go into the water right over there, down those old steps." He was executive vice-chancellor of the state college system when he took early retirement and moved to Avalon, and now he was hoping to help bring change without devastation.

Later I had a lunch of Catalina Island rock cod at Arno's and walked the mile back to Pebbly Beach for the three-o'clock plane. This time the pilot was younger and he wore a blue uniform with captain's epaulets. I wondered if the line was trying to modernize.

But as soon as we trundled down the ramp and into the water he reached down and noisily cranked up the wheels. We were back in the 1930s. I felt secure.

6
Hooray for Hollywood

MARILYN AND MAILER

"My God, she was sexy." "Very sexy, and very dead."

Never having seen Norman Mailer in the flesh, I went out to the Beverly Wilshire Monday evening for a cocktail reception given by the publishers of *Marilyn,* his new book on Marilyn Monroe.

I saw him standing just inside the entrance of the ballroom, facing a rapt little band of listeners. He stood in a slight crouch, feet apart, toes in, like a fighter; a good middleweight, over the hill, but game. His pale-blue eyes seemed alternately to burn and disconnect, as if his circuits were overloaded. He was more handsome than I would have thought from his pictures, and shorter. His hair was gray and frizzled.

"I had to lose weight," he was saying. "I was blowing up. I fasted for twenty days. Nothing but water. I went from one hundred eighty-three down to one hundred fifty."

"Twenty days! What did it do to you—psychologically?"

"I was fat, bilious, and hard on my wife. Your inner life deteriorates."

I moved on, leaving the author to a long hard evening. This was only the first round.

In the ballroom the early guests were milling over the deep rose carpet, examining a gallery of Marilyn Monroe photographs set up under the crystal chandeliers. There were dozens of Marilyns, some as familiar as Mona Lisa, some as fresh as life. Marilyn in the surf; Marilyn white against red in the famous calendar; Marilyn sitting up in bed for a kiss from Gable. Here and there among them were blowups of Mailer's words:

*... She was our angel, the sweet angel of sex, and the
sugar of sex came up from her like a resonance of sound
in the clearest grain of a violin. ...*

I drifted among the guests, catching a scrap of wisdom
here, a bit of gossip; a shaft, a puzzling fragment.

"My God, she was a sexy woman."

"Very sexy, and very dead."

"Mailer never met her, you know."

"Why the hell did he write the book?"

"He fell in love with her memory."

"He's a writer. He's going for the buck."

"If she were alive today she'd be—forty-odd. Decayed."

"Remember Housman? 'Smart lad, to slip betimes
away.' "

"This stuff sounds like it was written by her press agent."

"Yeh. Norman Mailer. Press agent for a dead star."

"One good thing, she won't have to pay him ten percent."

Up in the foyer a television crew was at work, its hot light
transfixing celebrities like moths. "And yet." Jack Lemmon
was telling a microphone, "she was not a great actress. The
greatest talent she had was to use what talent she did have to
the utmost. . . ."

"How does this compare," I asked a New York publisher,
"with a literary party in New York?"

"Very different. We'd consider that floodlight, all these
celebrities, kind of Hollywood. In New York at a party for
Mailer there would be only one celebrity—Mailer. There's
more décolletage here, too. In New York the women are a trifle
more dressed, a trifle more chic and a lot noisier."

A white-haired waiter came up with champagne on a silver tray. "Champagne?" he said. We took a glass and the waiter
smiled and moved on. "The waiters are nicer, too. In New
York, you'd get champagne, but the waiter wouldn't smile.
He'd throw it at you."

"Come meet Sam Jaffe," someone said and led me over to
a man who looked like a leaner Norman Mailer; older and
more secure, but astonishingly young for the high lama of the
original *Lost Horizon.*

"I saw *Lost Horizon* in Australia in 1937," I told him, "and
I thought you were dying then."

"That's what I always do," he said. "I die."

Jaffe was there at the start, the day Marilyn auditioned before John Huston for a part in a picture.

"Huston likes to doodle, you know. He was sitting there at the desk, doodling away, while Marilyn read her part. When she finished, Huston stood up to go, but Marilyn said she was going to do it over. He sat down and that time he listened. Afterwards he told me, 'That's the girl we want.'"

I sensed a current that goes through a party when a presence arrives. A stunning woman was standing on the threshold in a gown that exposed a wealth of suntanned flesh.

"Who's that?"

"Edy Williams. She's the wife of Russ Meyer, King of the Nudies. She's Mrs. King of the Nudies."

The party was supposed to be over at eight, but as I left I saw that Mailer was still on his feet, still sparring. He hadn't moved ten feet in two hours, closed in like a fighter in a ring. There were too many for him now; it was a rout. He was done for, but he still looked game.

So we think of Marilyn who was every man's love affair with America, Marilyn Monroe who was blond and beautiful and had a sweet little rinky-dink of a voice and all the cleanliness of all the clean American back yards. . . . She gave the feeling that if you made love to her, why then how could you not move more easily into sweets and the purchase of the full promise of future sweets, move into tender heavens where your flesh would be restored . . .

They had never met in life, and here he was now, revealing himself as her last, most passionate, most hopeless lover.

They seemed an odd couple: Mailer so open, Marilyn so closed. He should have called their book *The Naked and the Dead.*

THE ROSSLYN

"If you haven't been there for two weeks it's gone."

Hollywood has often been reported missing lately. I walked over to Fifth and Main the other morning and found part of it, at least, holed up in the defunct old Rosslyn Hotel.

Regina Gruss, a publicist for Boardwalk Productions, had phoned to tell me they were making a movie with a downtown location and had set up a sound stage in the Rosslyn lobby.

"I thought you might like to see it again," she said.

In a city as young and changing as Los Angeles, a man can become attached to any building older than he is. The Rosslyn was built in 1913, and until the Biltmore came along in the '20s, the Rosslyn and the Alexandria were downtown's best. It went dark in the '60s, though its newer annex across the street stayed on.

I couldn't find a way to get in. The Fifth Street entrance was a pants shop. A pawnbroker had the Main Street side. I walked down an alley and around to the back and saw the movie trucks and an open door. A red light was flashing. Somewhere inside they were shooting.

I tiptoed in and bumped into Miss Gruss. Talking in a whisper, she led me through cluttered service rooms to the murky lobby. The marble desk was intact. Lightless chandeliers hung from the vaulted ceiling. Up high the murals were in place, but time had turned their daylight into dusk.

At the center of the lobby under the Art Nouveau skylight sat a small house. We went in. Kitchen, living room, bedroom and bath. It had a spartan look. No pictures, no charm, no warmth.

"It looks like the 1950s," I said.

"It's Cooper's apartment," said Miss Gruss. "Actually, the time is now, but he can't get out of the past."

His windows, though, looked out at the night skyline of downtown Los Angeles 1973, an astonishing illusion created by the art director.

Cooper, Miss Gruss explained, is a onetime carney barker who has survived into middle age as the Organization's fixer in his seedy neighborhood. He sees his territory dying, his power fading and the young hoods closing in. He clings to memories of carney days and *The Nickel Ride*—the picture's name.

We climbed marble stairs to the open mezzanine. The rail was still red velvet. Props and power lines were all about. Robert Mulligan, the producer-director, was taking a break. This was his first experience with downtown Los Angeles.

"As soon as I pass La Cienega," he said, "I'm lost."

The movie was written for New York, but Mulligan decided that Fifth and Main looked enough like Tenth Avenue in the '50s. "Cheap bars and cheap restaurants and a mix of huge warehouses. All American cities look alike. This could be Cincinnati, Cleveland, St. Louis."

In Los Angeles, though, you had to make sure your location wouldn't be torn down in the middle of your schedule. "You turn a corner here and if you haven't been there for two weeks it's gone."

The dining room was off the mezzanine. In World War II it had become the downtown USO Canteen. It was never as glamorous as the Hollywood Canteen, where even Bette Davis danced with the boys from Iowa and Texas; but it was closer to Union Station, where lonely servicemen streamed in from the heartland twenty-four hours a day.

Miss Gruss led me out of the Rosslyn and east on Fifth Street to what appeared to be a new saloon. If there was anything East Fifth Street didn't need it was a new saloon. "It's a set," she said. "We built it. It used to be a barber college."

I had an idea a new saloon would get more attention in the neighborhood than a barber college. How many hungover winos would be huddled in its doorway at six o'clock in the morning, waiting for a mirage to open up?

We walked back to Main and turned the corner around the porny bookshop and descended a marble stairway to an enormous pool hall in the basement of a down-at-the-heels office building. The air was blue and musty. This was one of Cooper's hangouts too.

On the way back to my office I passed the Follies. When I was a boy they had a live orchestra, dazzling sets and a chorus of "80 girls 80." Now they were down to skin flicks and a couple of strippers.

My old turf had gone to hell. Oh, well, I thought, in two weeks it would probably be torn down.

HOLLYWOOD CEMETERY

"He was pure. There aren't any men like Tyrone Power
any more . . ."

A young woman with whom I have been slightly acquainted since she was in high school phoned the other day after returning from three weeks in Rome. We agreed it might be nice to have lunch.

"Is there someplace you'd like to go?" I asked.

"Do you know the Hollywood cemetery?"

"You mean out on Santa Monica Boulevard?" I said, thinking she knew of some little cafe nearby.

"Yes. Can you meet me by Douglas Fairbanks?"

"By Douglas Fairbanks?"

"You can't miss him. He's by the lake, next to the mausoleum."

"You mean you want to picnic in the cemetery?"

"We can. Or we could just meet there first."

I said it was perfectly agreeable, but it did seem odd enough to merit an explanation.

"I like cemeteries," she said. "They're fun. I go there lots of times. It's not morbid. It's nostalgia, you know, and history. Rudolph Valentino's there and Tyrone Power."

I agreed to meet her by Douglas Fairbanks. "You'll see my little blue car," she said.

I drove out Santa Monica and turned in through the gate. The place was almost deserted. A woman in a pink pantsuit was watering some flowers. A driver sat by a black hearse outside the chapel. In the distance a gardener was at work.

I found a blue Opel near the mausoleum. It was the only car in sight. In a moment I saw Carol Drummond walking toward me round a long ornamental pool.

"Hi," she said. Her hair was longer and more on the gold side than I remembered. In that setting, among the tombs, she looked especially young and alive, like the vision of some lyric poet.

She led me to the end of the pool, where a marble sarcophagus lay before a massive tablet in which was imbedded a bronze image of Douglas Fairbanks, with his vital dates and a graven inscription:

Good night, sweet prince,
And flights of angels lead thee to thy rest.

"Tyrone Power has the same quotation," said Miss Drummond. "He's over there. See that white bench? The first time I came here I sat on it and a gardener chased me off. He said it was Tyrone Power."

"Benches are to sit on," I said.

"Yes. I sit on it now. Usually I read Keats, or Shelley."

"It's gleaming white," I observed.

"Of course. He was pure. There aren't any men like Tyrone Power any more. He was a real swashbuckler."

There were three wilted carnations on the bench. "They must be two days old," Miss Drummond said. "Let's go see Rudolph Valentino."

She led me into the mausoleum and down a corridor lined with tiers of crypts and lighted dimly by stained-glass windows. We found the crypt.

Rodolfo Guglielmi Valentino
1895–1926

"It's very unpretentious," she said. "Why did he die so young?"

"Big cars and fast women," I said.

"And elevator shoes?" she suggested.

Outside again she led me to Cecil B. De Mille. There were two sarcophagi, side by side, circled by small family markers. It seemed unpretentious indeed for a man who might have erected the entire cemetery in a day, only to leave it on the cutting-room floor.

I wondered how Miss Drummond had become so interested in cemeteries.

"It was my senior year. I was taking this course in Los Angeles history and I found out how much history there is right here. Then when the earthquake came I was frightened, and I came out here and it relaxed me. It's so peaceful. There's never anyone here. I hope the tourists don't start coming in."

We took my car to Musso and Frank's for lunch and then went back to the cemetery to pick up hers. Shade had fallen over the Janss family monument and we sat there for a while, looking at her snapshots from Rome.

"This is Keats," she said, showing a tombstone. "You know who could have played Keats? Tyrone Power."

I would have thought Leslie Howard. I wonder where *he* is.

HOLLYWOOD PREMIERE

"She doesn't seem to have much on."
"She doesn't usually."

My old friend Jet Fore is one of the last of the old-style Hollywood press agents, so when he phoned me Monday and invited me to an old-style world premiere for a movie called *Cinderella Liberty*, I was overcome by nostalgia. I met Fore in the Marines in World War II and I've known him so long I can tell when he's telling the truth.

"It's going to be the world's first energy-crisis premiere," he said. "No klieg lights, to save power. All the press agents will be wearing miner's hats, with built-in lamps."

"Is that all?"

"Wait. The stars won't be arriving in limousines, like they used to. They'll be arriving by roller skates, dog sled, sedan chair, horse and buggy, camel and elephant. To save gas. Get it?"

"Who's going to be riding the elephant?" I was afraid they had turned out another one of those elephant-boy movies, in which case I wasn't going.

"Edy Williams. You remember Edy. She's UCLA's number-one football fan."

Yes, I remembered seeing Miss Williams flash her bare chest among the crowd for the TV cameras a time or two. Also, it was Miss Williams who had upstaged Norman Mailer at his literary cocktail party in the Beverly Wilshire.

The premiere was out at the Avco Center theater in West-wood. The scene was familiar. Red carpet, ropes, cops, one lane blocked off on Wilshire Boulevard. But no big lights. Jet Fore, in his miner's cap, was running the operation like a beach-master on a combat landing in the war.

Army Archerd, the perennial emcee, was there in a blue denim tuxedo, so I knew it was a genuine premiere. I was talking to Archerd when a leggy woman walked by in a short suede fur-trimmed coat.

"Hi, Army," she said. She flashed her coat open to reveal a blue T-shirt, which seemed to be all she was wearing. It was Miss Williams.

"She doesn't seem to have much on," I said.

"She doesn't usually," said Archerd with his customary poise.

My eyes followed Miss Williams. She walked back through the court and turned into the alley. I realized some-thing was awry. I found Jet Fore.

"Edy Williams is already here," I told him. "If she's com-ing on an elephant, how come she's already here?"

He looked hurt. "Jack, buddy," he said, "in thirty years, have I ever told you anything but lies?"

A man and woman skated by and vanished into the alley.

"Who were they?" I asked Fore.

"I don't know," he said. "Just some stars."

I walked back to the alley and down to the parking lot next door, behind Perpetual Savings. There was a horse trailer in the lot and a big truck-trailer stood at the curb with MOVIE-LAND ANIMALS painted on its side. I saw a horse and buggy, a camel and a small elephant, which Miss Williams was regard-ing speculatively. A girl with an elephant stick in one hand held the elephant by a tether. The elephant was restless. It nuzzled my chin and then started to untie my shoes.

"Where's the best place to ride?" Miss Williams asked.

"Back here," the girl said, tapping the elephant just above the tail.

I knew I ought to be getting back to the premiere, but my instincts told me the best part would be Miss Williams getting on the elephant.

I heard dogs barking and guessed that the dog sled had arrived out front. The two stars on roller skates took off, and then two more stars on a tandem bicycle. Jo Ann Pflug was carried off in a sedan chair, and for a moment I was torn between watching Miss Pflug get out of the sedan chair and watching Miss Williams get on the elephant.

"Well, here goes," said Miss Williams. The girl made the elephant kneel. Miss Williams whipped off her coat, threw it over the elephant's haunch and climbed on, a maneuver that revealed that under the blue T-shirt she was wearing a gold bikini.

I hurried out front to catch Miss Pflug, but by the time I could push through the crowd the premiere was over.

"It doesn't look to me like you saved much fuel," I said to Jet Fore afterward, "with all those trucks it took to get the animals here."

"Jack, boy," he said, "it was only symbolic. Get it?"

7

The Capital of Kitsch

THE GETTY MUSEUM AND THE ASSYRIAN RUBBER FACTORY

"Getty had indulged a billionaire's fancy and built himself a sand castle for his old age."

When the J. Paul Getty Museum opened in January there was more furor than fanfare, but in the four months since then it had been tumbled neither by earthquake nor criticism, and I thought it was safe enough to drive out the other afternoon for my first visit.

Getty had the museum built beside his mansion above Santa Monica Bay. A stone road climbs through towering evergreens to the world's most exotic underground garage. Nowhere but here has anything but a chariot ever been driven through such majestic gates.

As everyone must know by now, the museum is a re-creation, somewhat imaginative, of a luxurious Roman home, the Villa of the Papyri, which was buried by volcanic mud when Vesuvius obliterated the resort town of Herculaneum on the Bay of Naples in A.D. 79. The original villa remains underground to this day, but excavations have disclosed its plan and recovered many of its treasures.

From the garage an elevator rises to an airy colonnaded loggia that opens into the Peristyle Garden. The visitor need go no farther to decide whether he likes the museum or not. The garden is a hundred yards long, by my guess. A reflecting pool runs the full length, blue as the Bay of Naples. It lies in a formal garden planted with flowers, trees and shrubs said to have been fancied by the ancients. There is a bronze deer in the garden, bronze athletes, and at one end of the pool a bronze youth napping supine in the sun.

Along either side runs a deep portico with Doric columns, terrazzo floors, and walls painted to give the illusion of structures and landscapes beyond. At the north end of the garden stands the monumental façade of the museum with its row of eight Corinthian columns.

I wondered if a visitor in the days of the Villa of the Papyri might have been momentarily overpowered by such magnificence, as I was, and felt constrained to linger in the garden before approaching the great bronze doors. I sat on a stone seat and contemplated this extraordinary scene. Ever since I had turned into the stone road I'd been nervous. I was afraid I was going to like it, and I knew I shouldn't.

I had in mind the remarks of my esteemed friend William Wilson, in his preview of the museum last January. "L.A. intelligentsia, paranoid about our town's reputation as Kitsch City and the Plastic Paradise, will find that the Getty outstrips any existing monument to expensive, aggressive bad taste, cultural pretension and self-aggrandisement south of Hearst Castle. . . . Campier sensibilities who love playful theatrical artifice will delight in it as the funniest folly since the Assyrian rubber factory."

Wilson had exactly defined my dilemma. I'm paranoid about our town's reputation as Kitsch City, but I also love playful theatrical artifice. Sitting there in the garden, I had already lost touch with reality. I was a young Roman waiting for a tryst in the atrium with the youngest daughter of the villa's wealthy owner.

I could see the anguish of the intelligentsia. All that money might have gone into something of and for our own times. Instead, Getty had indulged a billionaire's fancy and built himself a sand castle for his old age. On the other hand, he had given us perennial schoolchildren a life-size model of a great structure that had not seen daylight since A.D. 79 and was likely to remain buried at Herculaneum for another 2,000 years. Besides, it was a structure that seemed to suit our Southern California coast. Those Romans had shown us something about building under warm skies by a warm sea.

I was swimming in these thoughts, below my depth, when

an elderly woman sat near me on the bench. In a moment she turned her head my way and looked me frankly in the eye.

"Do you like it?" she asked rather aggressively.

"Why, yes," I said without thinking. "I believe I do."

"I think it's just fantastic," she said.

"Yes," I said. "I do, too."

I walked back through the garden and down to the exotic garage to my car. I wasn't ready for the museum yet. The garden was enough for one day.

I'm afraid my case is hopeless. To tell the truth, I was a small boy when they built that Assyrian rubber factory, back in the era of wonderful nonsense, and I love it to this day.

I decided to drive out the freeway the other morning to make sure the factory was still there. I had seen it only a few weeks before, but in Los Angeles it is wise to search the landscape every morning, on arising. Our landmarks have a way of vanishing overnight, like baby teeth.

It was there, filling me once again with wonder. As a schoolboy, I had been on a tour of the plant; but that was only a hazy memory.

The Assyrian rubber factory is actually the Uniroyal rubber factory, on Telegraph Road a few blocks east of Atlantic Boulevard. It has a façade of perhaps a quarter mile; stone block walls with graven images and crenelated towers; and a central three-tiered ziggurat whose imperial doorway is guarded by two winged bulls with bearded human heads.

I might have been walking into antiquity, as well as my own childhood, as I entered under the bronze fretwork and found myself in a vaulted chamber with ancient reliefs carved in the walls and a colored frieze of chariots and kings.

"Can I help you?" asked a modern young woman at a reception desk.

I explained my mission, half expecting that no one in the factory would have the slightest idea about its origins. First, she pointed out a table on which a scroll, under glass, briefly told the story. Meanwhile, she said, "I'll see if I can reach anyone."

The factory, the scroll said, was a fanciful recreation of the great palace at Khorsabad, in ancient Babylonia. That one had been built nearly 3,000 years ago by the Assyrian King Sargon

II and had long since fallen into dust. This one, in whose entry hall I now stood, had been built in 1929 by Adolph Schliecher. Adolph Schliecher?

A young man came out to see me. He was Jacques Chatel, an engineer who was acting as curator of the factory's history and obviously enjoying it. Yes, it was still an object of much curiosity. In his office he showed me a letter from a Juan Fernando Velez, professor of architecture in Colombia, who had passed the factory on his way to Disneyland and was astonished, not surprisingly, to see this "rare Asirio-Babilonian" rubber factory. "I don't remember ever seeing anything like it," he added, a statement whose honesty could not be doubted.

Adolph Schliecher? Schliecher was the founder of the Samson Tire & Rubber Company, and in 1929, when UCLA was raising medieval palaces at Westwood, Schliecher reached much farther back into time for his rubber plant. In 1930 he sold Samson to the United States Rubber Company (now Uniroyal) and busied himself with good works.

Uniroyal doesn't mind being a curiosity piece, said Chatel, and welcomes the scrutiny of scholars and serious students. There are no guided tours, however, as inside those ancient walls there is nothing but a modern tire factory. You can see it all, if you like, by turning off the freeway at Washington or Atlantic and driving slowly by on the way to visit relatives or Disneyland.

J. Paul Getty died the other day at eighty-three, a billionaire, and when a man is that old and that rich, it may not be too cynical to guess that not everyone who had done business with him was sorry to see him go. But I was.

Mr. Getty had invited me to lunch, and now it's too late to accept.

That Mr. Getty and I had been involved in business dealings was not widely known. Billionaires, as we have seen, tend to be secretive, and for me to talk would have been indiscreet if not impertinent. For in a rather modest way Mr. Getty was a patron of mine.

Evidently I first came to Mr. Getty's attention in November 1974 when *Westways* magazine published an article of mine on the J. Paul Getty Museum at Malibu, which Mr. Getty built at a cost of seventeen million dollars, supervising its design and construction almost stone by stone from Sutton Place, his seventy-two-room Tudor mansion in Surrey, England.

But critics of art and architecture generally deplored the museum as kitsch and reproached its creator for wasting millions on a structure designed for another place and time, by an architect two thousand years in his grave. Mr. Getty was accused of taking vanity to the point of folly if not madness. He had built a sand castle for his second childhood.

But I liked it, and said so. Perhaps I'm in my second childhood too. "As I sat there on that ancient stone bench," I wrote in the article, "I surrendered to the illusion. The sky was blue. A slow wind came up from the bay, moving through the surrounding screen of pine, eucalyptus, sycamore and cypress. The bronze youth dozing in the pool was a slave; he would soon be awakened by his master's whistle. It was a nice day in Herculaneum, summer of '74."

Some time later I heard from Stephen Garrett, director of the museum. Mr. Getty had read the article. He liked it. He wanted to buy the reprint rights. He wanted to have it on sale in the museum's bookshop. What were my terms?

I was deeply pleased. A second sale of something he has already written is manna to any writer, and it was especially gratifying to have one's work coveted by the world's richest man. But what should I charge him? I was not used to dealing with anyone that rich.

I was tempted to make a debonair gesture and tell Mr. Getty he could have the rights for nothing. After all, I was a patron of the arts too. He had donated the museum, and I was sure it would bring pleasure to millions of people; why shouldn't I donate a few words?

On the other hand, if I *gave* him the rights, I wouldn't be able to say that I had actually negotiated a business deal with J. Paul Getty. No, that wouldn't do. I had to receive *some* money, if only a token. But if I charged more than he wanted to pay, I might drive him out.

I explained my dilemma to Garrett. Transatlantic negotiations began. My position of course had to be conveyed to Mr. Getty by telephone, and vice versa, with Garrett in the middle. There were one or two hitches. At first the Getty interests misinterpreted what must have seemed to them an equivocal if not incomprehensible stance on my part and got the impression that I wanted to give the rights to Mr. Getty free of charge. I clarified my position, and in a few weeks the wrinkles were ironed out. I received a final letter from Garrett, which said, in part: "We are most grateful for your cooperation in this matter and have enclosed a token of our appreciation. We will, as earlier discussed, be selling the reprint at cost in the Museum Bookstore." The token was a check for two hundred dollars.

That was in November 1975. In December I received a letter from Sutton Place, Guildford, Surrey, as follows:

> *Dear Mr. Smith:*
>
> *My associates in Los Angeles have advised me that they understand you might be coming to London in the early part of 1976. If you do come I would be delighted if you would come and have lunch with me at Sutton Place.*
>
>
>
> *Yours sincerely,*
> J. PAUL GETTY
>

Mr. Getty never saw his sand castle. He had not been home to Malibu for twenty years. The staff at the museum always expected him to drop in, any day, any minute. Once a helicopter had hovered over the garden and one of the gardeners had been quite sure it was Mr. Getty looking down from it. But it wasn't, and when they flew him home at last, he was dead.

THE PINK LADY

"They stood on her ears, her lips, her shoulders, her bosom, her hips, her knees."

I am disconsolate that I didn't get to see the irreverent sculpture that stood for a few hours last Friday morning in the reflecting pools of the Department of Water and Power building in the civic center.

The first I knew of its brief life was when I brought the paper in on Saturday morning and saw the picture on the front page. It showed three men in hip boots pulling down the sculpture in front of a gallery of civic center workers whose mood could only be guessed at.

The story said the work of art had sprouted overnight in the pool, describing it as "a three-pronged, serpentine, green-bronze hollow beanstalk topped by orange and yellow lotuses which alternately lighted up and spouted water."

In the picture the "sprouts" looked about three times as tall as the men in hip boots. They were thicker at the bottom, growing thinner, like elephant trunks thrusting up out of the water and balancing the lotus blossoms, as big as washtubs, at the top. They reminded me of that remarkable creation of the Baja desert, the boojum tree, which also resembles an elephant's trunk with a flower at the top.

I am disconsolate, as I say, that I was not there Friday morning when these insouciant intruders were discovered, alternately lighting up and spouting water, by DWP employees showing up for another day's work.

As the story in the paper said, some of them welcomed the spouting lotuses as "the most exciting thing to happen around there since the energy shortage," and they must have been disappointed when, long before the sun was overhead, the maintenance crew waded into the pool and stolidly began their nihilistic task.

It was inevitable. The sculpture after all was contraband. It was installed by its creator and his helpers in dark of night, and its presence was not only an affront to the dignity of the DWP but a breach of the standard committee procedures by which works of art are procured in a proper bureaucracy.

The picture of the workmen executing their cheerless assignment, while the crowd hung back, too prudent to protest, reminded me sharply of the Pink Lady affair of a few years ago.

The Pink Lady, you may remember, was a nude woman, sixty feet high, who appeared at dawn one morning, very much like the sprouting lotuses, on a sheer rock cliff above a tunnel on Malibu Canyon Road.

She was exuberant and free. One hand clutched a sprig of wildflowers and her long dark tresses flowed backward as she gamboled across the rock, nude and pink as a rose.

To a populace worn ragged by bad news and worse politics,

the Pink Lady was a refreshment, a symbol of uninhibited joy. In twenty-four hours she was a *cause célèbre*. Cars gorged the roadside for a half mile back from the tunnel. Crowds gawked, wondering at the nerve and skill of the anonymous artist. They took movies and snapshots and argued about art and morality. The Pink Lady's message, said the editorial page of the *Times*, was *"toujours gai."*

But of course she was illegitimate; a witch. She had to go. They set the fire department on her first, but the Pink Lady was not to be easily exorcised. High-power hoses failed to dissolve her. Paint remover only turned her pinker. The first day's assault ended in darkness and humiliation.

They were back the next morning, trampling on leaflets describing them as "brutal, sadistic, prudish, inartistic and Victorian." In the end, they had to send men up the cliff in alpine harness to paint the lady out with spray guns. Like insects they stood on her ears, her lips, her shoulders, her bosom, her hips, her knees, inch by inch masking her flesh until at last she was only a pink shadow of herself.

Like the Pink Lady, the civic center lotus sculpture was an irresistible outcropping of joy in a joyless time. The godfathers of the DWP, seeking to set an example for a simple-minded public in the energy crisis, had turned off their own lights and fountains and taken to public acts of asceticism like Hindu fakirs.

Is it any wonder that now and then the frustrated cockroach in us cries out *"toujours gai,* Mehitabel, *toujours gai!"*?

THE MILLION-DOLLAR JUKEBOX

" 'What do you think?' 'Very mixed,' she said."

It was the kind of late-April day we often have in January, so I walked over to the new mall during the noon hour to hear the Triforium.

I had no intention of taking sides in the controversy which has so far made more noise than its subject. But the thing was there, for better or worse. I had seen it from time to time during its construction, and I wanted to hear it perform. After all, if you pay a dollar for a whistle, you want to hear it whistle; and we had paid nearly a million for the Triforium.

I cut through the old City Hall park and crossed Main Street and walked north toward Temple until I picked up the signal. Someone was singing "Sunrise, Sunset." I went in on the beam.

There were perhaps eighty people in Bowron Square, where the Triforium was singing away. They sat around it on the walls, or on the few benches, eating lunch or reading or simply listening. I sat on the wall in front of the Triforium near a woman who sat alone. She wore a plastic JUROR button on the jacket of her pantsuit.

A smart little breeze was rippling the pool underneath the Triforium and the jacaranda trees around the square. The sky was pure.

I studied the Triforium, wondering at the epithets it had already inspired. The Psychedelic Nickelodeon. The Million-Dollar Firefly. The Million-Dollar Jukebox.

It looked something like three six-story tuning forks standing in a small circle and leaning slightly in toward each other, with a crown of red, orange, amber, green and blue junk jewelry. It was from these glass gauds, I assumed, that the sound was emanating.

No, on second thought, its three elements resembled something else more than tuning forks. Wishbones? Yes. Three wishbones in search of a turkey. Or had they already found their turkey?

"Sunrise, Sunset" came to an end, and in a moment the thing began to play a familiar tune, on the piano. "Baa Baa Black Sheep, Have You Any Wool?" with elegant variations. If I wasn't mistaken, it was Mozart's variations on a nursery rhyme. If it wasn't Mozart, it was certainly "Baa Baa Black Sheep." To me, it was delightful. Simple, lively, crisp, nostalgic. And the thing didn't play bad piano, either.

I caught the juror's eye. "What do you think?" I asked, sensing that she too had been trying to appraise the instrument in front of us.

"Very mixed," she said after a moment.

I nodded. "Me too."

She seemed to be in deliberation, trying to be fair. Finally she said, "I don't see why it had to cost that much."

I knew she was going to be a good juror.

Two of our ubiquitous yellow school buses drew up across the street and a platoon of children infiltrated the square and took up positions on a wall in a more or less orderly row. They were all assiduously eroding their dental enamel by masticating multicolored jumbo suckers which looked like miniature Triforiums.

A man got up from a nearby bench and I walked over to take the empty seat. There was a woman at the other end, doing needlepoint. She had almost finished the piece in hand.

Mozart came to an end and then there was something I could define only as soul music, followed by something that might have been rock, but not very hard.

"I thought I was going to hear a concert," the woman on the bench beside me volunteered, "but not rock 'n' roll."

She had been on jury duty two days but hadn't been seated yet and was looking forward with reluctance to the prospect of sitting in a jury room for thirty days with nothing to do. "I'm not used to doing nothing," she said. "It's driving me up the wall."

I suggested that it must help to have this little square to escape to, at least on the lunch hour.

"Oh, it's a lovely place to sit out. And when you think it's the middle of January!"

The music turned soft again. Something symphonic, with lots of violins and cellos.

"That sounds like a Beethoven tune," the juror said. "I can take anything but Wagner. He's got too heavy a hand."

She put her needlepoint away and set out to do her duty. I headed back for the office.

I'd have to say I enjoyed the interlude. If I have a complaint, outside of the thing's cost, it would be that it's making a mistake trying to please everybody all at once. It ought to play a classical concert one day, jazz the next, pop the next, and so on.

I won't enter my final judgment until I hear it do the Ninth Symphony on a windy day in March. But no Wagner. Wagner's too heavy-handed for me, too.

8

On the Waterfront

ARRIVALS AND DEPARTURES

"Cut to Veronica Lake at the ship's rail . . ."

"During a dream on the couch after dinner tonight, I started browsing through the Ship Movements in the *Times*. I made my selections of the ships that held the most fascination for me. What names! What destinations!"

Thus began a letter from Duke Russell. I have never met Russell, though he lives nearby in Hollywood, but I am grateful for his occasional letters, which are sometimes wry, sometimes nostalgic, sometimes pure fantasy.

This time he had enclosed the Ship Movements chart from the *Times* of January 23, a daily feature that appears back on the vital-statistics page and is ignored, I'm sure, by all but a very few readers.

Most of us have noticed it only in the movies. You know the scene. There is a closeup of Vessels Due to Arrive Today. Alan Ladd runs a finger down the list and stops at the *Asia Maru*, due at noon from Tokyo. Cut to Veronica Lake at the ship's rail and Ladd in the crowd on the wharf, looking up. Miss Lake is an international jewel thief, with a cache of emeralds in her luggage, and Ladd is a T-man. Ever since that steamy night in Rangoon, when he was with the CIA, he's been crazy about her, especially the way that hank of yellow hair falls over one eye, but if you think that will keep him from doing his duty, you don't know our Ladd.

Looking down the list of vessels in port or arriving on January 23, Duke Russell imagined himself boarding the *China Sea*, out of New Orleans, and running into Peter Lorre, Sidney

Greenstreet and Humphrey Bogart. W. C. Fields was the captain and not entirely sober.

Russell's game may seem childish for grown men, but when I was a boy I used to hitchhike down to San Pedro and walk along the wharfs and sometimes actually go aboard some creaking freighter whose crew was probably tying one on in Shanghai Red's on Beacon Street, and whose captain was holed up in his cabin, drinking gin and scheming with Sidney Greenstreet. The captain was Oscar Homolka.

I suppose that with today's obsession with security, a boy would never be allowed up a gangway, or even near one; but nobody ever seemed to mind me. I trailed my fingers over teakwood rails; looked into holds that reeked of copra; held my breath as I encountered sinister-looking deck hands in sarongs and headbands.

Sometimes I even had the cheek to board some big white liner, in for the day from Hong Kong, its engines breathing softly below as it got up steam for an imminent departure. Once I passed through a grand saloon and caught sight of a ruddy gentleman in a Norfolk jacket and tweed plus fours, sitting in a rattan deck chair and peering at me over his newspaper with the face of Rudyard Kipling. It wasn't Kipling, of course, but it was someone I knew; someone I had met, no doubt, through a mutual acquaintance named Somerset Maugham.

I watched them cast off and move slowly down channel on their way out to the romantic destinations whose names were lettered on their sterns . . . *Singapore* . . . *London* . . . *Cristóbal* . . .

I knew that one day I would sail on one of those departing vessels, and one day I did. If Miss Lake was aboard, however, I never knew it. As a galley hand, I spent most of my time at sea below the waterline.

I don't know if the harbor holds any fascination for boys today. Possibly not, with jets that take you to London while you watch Clint Eastwood. And anyway the streets of Rangoon would be clogged with Datsuns and Toyotas.

But I looked back through the paper to the Ship Movements just this morning and they are still arriving and departing . . . *Bristol Clipper* out of Guayaquil . . . *Montego* out of Hong Kong . . . *Royal Viking Sea* out of Mazatlán . . .

But it's only geezers like me and Russell, I suppose, who know that Bogart and Lorre and Greenstreet and Veronica are also arriving and departing.

SHANGHAI RED

"He ran the roughest waterfront bar in the world and boasted he could lick any man in the joint."

Okinawa, Japan

Dear Mr. Smith

On reading your always interesting column in the *Okinawa Morning Star* recently, I noted that you made reference to Shanghai Red's saloon in Pedro. Is that old son of a gun still around after all these years?

I remember well how he would always stick a lighted cigarette behind his ear rather than bother with an ashtray. I have had many cool ones in his place years back when I was shipping out of the West Coast in the old outfits—Dollar Lines, Luckenback, Hawaiian-American. Able seamen made $28.50 a month and a guy with five bucks could live like a king on the beach in Yokohama for a month.

I haven't been on the waterfront in Pedro since '42, so I imagine that things have changed more than somewhat. I quit sailing in '40, enlisted in the Marine Corps, did 24 and retired out here in '64.

If Red is still in business and you ever get out that way, have a cool one for me.

Cordially yours,
L. F. Smith
(Texas City Smitty)
Gunnery Sg. USMC (ret.)

Dear Gunny:

Shanghai Red, I'm sorry to tell you, died in June 1957. That's nearly seventeen years ago, and what saddens me almost as much as Red's being gone so long is the fact that I wrote his obituary. I hate to believe it was that long ago.

Just to refresh my memory I dug out the clipping and I thought you might like to know some of the facts about Red. Every able drinking seaman who hit San Pedro washed up in Red's saloon, but all they knew about Red was that he ran the roughest waterfront bar in the world, boasted he could lick any man in the joint and was a soft touch for any sailor who had been rolled or lost his pay in a crap game or was otherwise momentarily embarrassed.

His real name was Charles Oliver Eisenberg and he was born on San Francisco's Barbary Coast, where he learned his trade early as bar boy in a waterfront dive. When he was old enough, or maybe before, he joined the Navy and saw the world. He went back to the land again in Shanghai and bought into a waterfront saloon. That's where he earned his name. When he had a stake he came home and opened up on Beacon Street.

The day Red died they padlocked his doors and the place never opened again. Some years ago the whole street was condemned for a redevelopment project. It has been dragging on so long that when I got your letter I wondered if Red's old bucket of blood might still be there. I was in the neighborhood the other day and drove over to the street for a look.

Yes, Gunny, times have changed more than somewhat. Shanghai Red's was on the northwest corner of Fifth and Beacon, as I remember. It's gone, along with every other brick that stood on Beacon between Fourth and Sixth, both sides of the street. Every flophouse, laundry, chop suey joint, greasy spoon, bail bond office, dance hall, steambath and pawnshop.

They haven't started to build anything new yet. The way it's going we might not see it this century. It's just four square blocks laid bare. We are having an early spring, though, and the ground is weed-grown up to your knees, green and fresh as a meadow.

The block between Sixth and Seventh, on the west side across the street from the big city building where they used to have the police station, is still standing, but it looks like a beaten old fighter sagging on the ropes. I saw some men in hard hats on the roof of the walk-up hotel on the corner of Sixth, smashing away at the top of its walls with sledgehammers, and a man in a powerlift was running around below like a Dodge-em driver on the Pike, scooping up fallen bricks. The police station is gone. Beacon Street doesn't need much law any more.

I just thought you might like to know, Gunny, and if you ever hit Pedro again, I don't know where you're going to find an honest man and an honest drink.

Semper fi
Jack Smith

THE OCEAN VIEW HOTEL

*"Aimee triumphed, having ruined a grand jury, a deputy
D. A., a police captain and a judge."*

I went out to Venice the other morning to look at the old Ocean View Hotel. For years, like the rest of old Venice, it had been sinking into a tacky senility. The lobby had grown dim and seedy. There seemed to be no people in it, just shabby bundles sitting in tired chairs and staring out through misty windows at nothing.

The w had long since fallen from the sign over the door, thus altering OCEAN VIEW to OCEAN VIE, a cruel Gallic joke.

I found the door locked, but a caretaker opened up. He looked close to eighty and hardly more than five feet tall.

"Mr. Woo said you'd show me around," I told him.

"Yes, yes," he said. "Come on in. It's all finished now."

The lobby looked brand new. Over the elevator door a message had been spelled out for the tenants yet to come: "You will do foolish things, but do them with enthusiasm."
—Coletto.

"Could I see the second floor?" I asked.

He took me up to the second floor in the elevator and I walked down the fresh hall over a bright new carpet to one of the suites with a bay window looking out over Ocean Front Walk to the sea.

I thought back to my recent conversation with Young Woo, a neighbor of ours on Mt. Washington. He had stopped by our house at eight o'clock in the morning, rather in a state of excitement. If we had been closer friends I might have thought he had just become a father again. But I'd met him only once before, when he had come by with young Tim Johnson and sold me four sacks of steer manure for the YMCA. I hoped it wasn't manure again.

"You know the Ocean View Hotel?" he began. "In Venice?"

For a year, he said, he and his company, Urbatec, had been restoring the Ocean View as an apartment hotel for low-income elderly tenants. They had reinforced it with steel, remodeled it throughout, peeled off the glazed white brick façade and put it back again, replacing lost or broken bricks with handmade copies. It had cost a million dollars, with federal and city assistance. The final inspection was due that day.

For Woo, it had been a labor of love. They could have torn down the hotel and built a new one for a million dollars, but they had wanted to save the old building, not only for its character but also for its history. "It was where Aimee McPherson stayed," he said. "You know?"

Yes. It was in her ocean-view room on the second floor that Aimee had changed into her bathing suit before walking out across the beach and—as the world was to think—drowning in the sea. That was on May 18, 1926.

For Los Angeles newspapers, which enjoyed an abundance of bizarre news stories in that exuberant era, it was the most bizarre of all. It held page one for weeks, while tens of thousands of Sister Aimee's followers flocked to the beach to await her resurrection.

Then, five weeks later, at one o'clock in the morning, she appeared in the Mexican border town of Agua Prieta and told a breathtaking tale of being kidnaped and held captive in an adobe shack and of escaping and walking twenty miles across the desert.

The Second Coming could hardly have inspired more hosannas; a hundred thousand people lined Aimee's route from the station to Angelus Temple. The Fire Department band played "Praise God from Whom All Blessings Flow" and the temple choir sang "Wonderful Savior." But the police sulked, wondering about Aimee's unscuffed shoes and buoyant health, and bit by bit they concluded that Sister Aimee had spent those weeks at a cottage in Carmel with her temple's virile radio engineer.

The law moved ponderously to bring Aimee to earth, but in the end she triumphed, having ruined a grand jury, a deputy D. A., a police captain and a judge and having canonized herself as the most charismatic figure in the nation west of Texas Guinan.

"This old building will never come down now," the caretaker said as we looked out the bay window over Aimee's beach.

Good, I thought. Let Angelus Temple stand a thousand years as a memorial to Sister Aimee's evangelical spirit. This old hotel would stand as a memorial to her very human flesh. She might have done a foolish thing, but she did it with enthusiasm.

Vive l'Ocean Vie.

9

Effervescent Days

COUNTY LANDFILL NO. 4

*" 'That,' I said out loud as the hats flew,
'is probably a mistake.' "*

Spring must have come late to County Landfill No. 4, also known as the Scholl Canyon dump. The road to the dump rises through the hills above Eagle Rock, and I found the wildflowers, weeds and bushes in full bloom when I drove up with a load of trash.

It was early Monday morning, the dump being closed on Sunday. I had started cleaning out the garage over the weekend, and this was my first load of nonbiodegradable debris. I was cleaning out the garage for the last time, I had promised myself, and was determined that this time everything must go, including the sentiment that had caused us to accumulate so much junk in the first place.

The road trembled under the huge rubbish trucks grinding their way up to the landfill site and back. It was a mile or two from North Figueroa Street to the summit, where the weigh-in station stands beside a small green oasis. I pulled up behind an enormous white truck and another one pulled up behind me. It was a thrill, driving my little green minitruck up there with the big boys.

I paid my two dollars and followed the white truck down into the canyon, a mile or so, to a vast raw ravine where half a dozen commercial rubbish trucks and two or three smaller ones, like mine, were backed up to the trash line disgorging their loads.

At the far end of the line two bulldozers were attacking the waves of trash deposited by trucks which, I supposed, had only recently departed. The dozers charged the line and shoved the trash up toward a terrace where a monstrous machine seemed to be grinding it into the landscape. There was an air of urgency about the operation; of combat. It reminded me of a beachhead in World War II. One had best unload fast and get the hell out.

I backed up beside a pickup which two men were emptying of an assortment of threadbare white elephants not much different from my own—two chairs and a sofa whose cheap gold upholstery had ruptured here and there to let their cheap insides ooze out; a child's bicycle; a set of bedsprings, an enameled laundry tub, apparently in good condition; a push-type lawnmower.

I had a sense of one-upmanship as I horsed our old power mower out of my truck and heaved it into the waste, but my neighbors didn't notice. It gave me a twinge when the doughty old mower sank into the morass. The irony of it was that the thing still worked. It was something like shooting a horse.

Quickly I unloaded the rest—the swag lamps, the chaise longue, the barbecue, the old tires, the wheel, a carton of my wife's Gatsby hats. "That," I said out loud as the hats flew, "is probably a mistake."

It occurred to me that I stood at the very end of civilization's treadmill. The theologians and philosophers might talk in solemn abstractions of man's ultimate function; I was out here doing it.

I felt lighthearted and unburdened as I drove up out of the dump and back down the road. Now and then a view of the city would flash through a gap in the hills. The flowers were so abundant and varied that I pulled off the road to pick a few, hoping it wasn't against the rules, like salvage.

In a few minutes, taking only one sprig of each variety, I had a poppy with a yellow center and pure white petals as big as my hand; a small pale purple aster; a ruby-red oleander; a sticky monkey flower like an orange trumpet; a yellow Spanish broom; a mint with tiny purple-tipped white flowers; and three or four others I couldn't name.

As I drove on down the hill, the bouquet beside me on the seat, I reflected that every member of the affluent society ought to take a load of his trash to the dump at least once a

year, preferably in the spring. One day the waste I had left
behind up there in the canyon would be part of a landfill on
which grass and trees would grow and children would play. It
was like taking part in God's Creation.

That evening when my wife came home from work she
found the wildflowers in a bowl on the bar.

"They're exquisite," she said. "Where did they come
from?"

"I picked them for you," I told her, "on the road to the
dump."

She was so touched she forgave me for throwing out her
hats.

THE UNIVERSAL TOUR

*" 'Part, Red Sea!' the guide chanted. 'Come on,
everyone say it!' "*

To complete my research on a certain project, I went out
to Universal Studios in the hills above Burbank the other
morning to see the Red Sea part. I had already taken the guided
tour of the studios, but that was before they put in the parting
of the sea, and I felt it was something I couldn't afford to
ignore.

I was hoping simply to buy a ticket and watch that one
miracle, without having to take the whole tour over again, but
you can't do that. So I climbed aboard a three-car tram and
went the route. It takes two and a half hours.

Our guide was a young man who stood at the front of the
first car and diverted us with a nonstop commentary as we
rolled past warehouses, dressing rooms, sound stages and
false-front towns.

"How many came to see a movie star today?" he asked
with an enthusiasm that proved tireless, if unfounded. There
was a showing of hands. "Well, we're surrounded by dressing
rooms here, so if you happen to see someone you recognize,
feel free to *stare* at that person. Oh, and be sure to yell out his
name, so everybody else can see him. But don't *attack* him."

He told about the time they had seen Robert Redford. "Fifty ladies jumped out and began chasing him." Seeking sanctuary, Redford had run into a men's room, thinking the ladies wouldn't pursue him there. "But they did. Fifty ladies, right into the men's room."

A minute later he pointed out a large gray building on our right. "That's the building where the men's room was," he said.

We passed a row of dressing rooms with names on the doors. Julie Harris. Robert Young. Dennis Weaver.

"That's Dennis Weaver's little car there," the guide said. "The little orange one."

All heads turned toward the little orange car in front of Dennis Weaver's dressing room.

The tram halted at the dressing room that had been built for Lana Turner when she did *Madame X* and which now was used by Lucille Ball. It was a gray cottage with a tiny yard and trees all around. We had to wait for the tour ahead of us to get through the dressing room before we could go in, and our guide told us we could sit in the shade under a cluster of trees off to one side. "But those are real birds in those trees," he warned, "so you sit there at your own risk."

While we waited he took a count. Anybody from foreign countries? Three: Australia, Canada, Norway. Other states? Nevada, Virginia, Wisconsin, Nebraska, Illinois, Ohio, Arkansas, Indiana, North Carolina and one or two others I didn't catch. I wondered what people from Australia, Canada, Norway and all those Midwestern states would think of a place where it had to be pointed out to you that the birds in the trees were real.

"That might be Edith Head over there," the guide said. "She has a car like that. . . . No . . . it's not Edith Head."

A minute later. "Folks, the man in the gray suit is Mr. Dan Fraser, from the *Kojak* series."

We watched Mr. Dan Fraser walk by, evidently on a lunch break.

"And there's Mr. Mark Russell from the *Kojak* series."

Mr. Russell stopped to smile and wave and two women dashed to his side, one evidently the mother-in-law, while the husband took a snapshot.

In this excitement I think I may have been the only one to notice a little blue car that went humming by with TELLY SAVALAS lettered on the side. Mr. Telly Savalas wasn't in it, though.

The tour was almost over before we came to the Red Sea. It was the same old lake they had for the ocean in *McHale's Navy.* They hadn't even dyed it red. The tram pulled up to a narrow neck of the water.

"Part, Red Sea!" the guide chanted. "Come on, everyone say it! Part, Red Sea!"

There was a sound of water being sucked down a drain, and a trough appeared in the water, deepening between two walls until it bottomed out at a metal roadway and the tram trundled on through.

I was disappointed. I had hoped to hear God's voice, something like soft thunder, I imagined it would be. Or at least Charlton Heston's voice. Or his stand-in's voice. It seemed to me that if C. B. De Mille could get God to talk for *The Ten Commandments,* Jules Stein should be able to get Charlton Heston for the Universal tour. Or at least his stand-in. When you're all set for God, it's a letdown to hear some tour guide give the command, "Part, Red Sea!"

LAKE HOLLYWOOD

"If you hear us hollering, hide behind a tree."

On a tip from a reader I drove up to Lake Hollywood early the other morning in search of "the therapeutic sound of rushing waters, the singing of hundreds of birds and the wind in the pine trees."

I not only found these things, as promised, but I may also have played a bit part in a movie called *Earthquake.*

The gate to the road that runs around the lake was open, but a guard was there to tell motorists the road was blocked. "They're shooting a movie back there," he said.

I set out to walk it. In less than a minute I might have been in the High Sierra, except for the road itself and the twelve-foot steel fence screening it off from the lake. The lake-shore was so thickly forested that only now and then did the lake show through. The air was scented with eucalyptus and pine. I heard nothing but mourning doves and a distant barking dog. How pretty the world would be, I thought, if only we could build a fence around it and keep people out.

I must have walked a mile before I met another person—a woman in a quilt-patch coat with a small shaggy dog. She was walking toward me, throwing a red rubber ball for the dog to fetch.

"Good morning," she said.

"Hello," I said. "You have a very smart dog there."

"Thank you."

Farther on I met a very pretty young woman in a long purple skirt with a blue jacket and a floppy yellow hat. "Hello," I said. She gave me a guarded smile and hurried on, silent as an Indian. When they don't have a dog it's hard to strike up a conversation.

The movie company was down at the end of the lake by the dam: a bus, a snack wagon, two or three portable dressing rooms, power equipment. People idling about, waiting calls. At the end of the dam they had built a set, a small two-story structure. A man with a bullhorn stood on a platform looking over a camera into the upper room. "Quiet," he called. Then: "All right, roll it. Action."

Suddenly there was a rumbling, deep and unnerving, exactly the sound of an earthquake. The upstairs room appeared to be shaking. In a moment the door was yanked open and two men hurried out and down the steps.

"Cut!" the director shouted.

I didn't know the story, but I guessed that the dam breaks in the earthquake and Hollywood is wiped out. I started to walk across the dam and complete my tour of the lake.

"Sir," a man said, catching up to me. "Please don't go that way. We're shooting right out there over the dam, through the window."

I saw his point. They wouldn't want a man walking casually across the dam just when it was about to go. I moved back to wait until they had the scene wrapped up. But it wasn't going well. Six more times they shot it, and still the director wasn't satisfied.

I saw a path below the dam, with a heavy cover of pines, and asked the man if I could go that way. He studied the angle. "All right," he said, "but if you hear us hollering, hide behind a tree."

I took off down the trail. Suddenly I heard a shout and looked back and saw that I had a clear view of the window. That meant, then, that the camera shooting through the window had a clear view of me.

I ran off the trail into the cover of the trees and walked over a carpet of pine needles in the filtered light. When I reached the far end of the dam, I found myself blocked off from the road by the fence. I would have to go back.

I hiked back to the set, keeping under cover, and by then they had finished the scene and were taking a break. I hurried across the dam and walked on around the lake, my legs telling me it was about three miles.

Who knows? If I do turn up in that scene the director just might keep me in. It would add a dramatic touch, a man walking under the dam as the earthquake strikes. Maybe they'll even put me in the credits, the way they sometimes do with a bit player. "Walking man," or "Man in tan jacket."

If so, I would like them to know that the man was me and that my name, for theatrical purposes, is J Clifford Smith. I think it has more class.

10

Creatures Great and Small

WHALE WATCH

" 'Two pilot whales,' said the steadfast Meyerdierks."

For five hours one afternoon I felt somewhat like an astronaut, riding in a capsule free of earth.

I was one of six passengers on the Goodyear Blimp *Columbia*, floating over San Pedro Channel and Catalina Island in search of the great gray whale.

It was one of the several flights in the annual Whalewatch Operation of the American Cetacean Society, a nonprofit group dedicated to the welfare of marine life, especially whales, dolphins and porpoises.

My fellow passengers were an oceanographer, a political science professor, a Smithsonian mammalogist and a husband-wife team from the ACS and the Audubon Society. I don't know why I was included in such an elite group, unless it was my unusual work in bird identification.

Soon after we climbed into the little car under the 192-foot blimp the ground crew let go the lines, the pilot gunned the engines and we scudded off as gently as a cloud.

The Goodyear base is inside the elbow of the harbor and San Diego freeways, and from a thousand feet up the panorama was a graphic sermon on the wages of a mechanized civilization. Steel power-line towers; oil-tank storage farms; enormous factories with even larger aprons of parked cars like the beaded skirts of the Jazz Age.

We soared over the Palos Verdes Peninsula, looking down on the other side of the coin. Green estates; baronial houses with stables and tennis courts and turquoise pools; wooded avenues and airy schoolyards, all encircled by an uncluttered lacy seashore.

"California gull," said Herman Meyerdierks. He was on my right at the rear of the car, looking earthward through binoculars.

"How many?" said Bettey Meyerdierks, on my left.

"One."

It was our first sighting of wildlife. The Meyerdierkses had come along to keep count. "He observes," she said, "and I write."

One sea gull was not an exciting start, but we soon added to the list. "Nineteen ringtailed gulls," said Meyerdierks. I wondered how he knew there were nineteen. "He estimates," said Mrs. Meyerdierks.

It was not a brilliant day. The sky was pearly. The ocean had the nap of a good English tweed. Below us nothing moved —not a boat, not a fish. It was a waste.

"One shearwater gull," said Meyerdierks after a while.

Then: "There! Down there!" shouted someone, pointing down on our starboard quarter. The men up forward crowded to the windows and looked down at what seemed at first only a flattening-out of the water. Then two shapes appeared under the surface, long and cigar-shaped, of a pale-green color like ancient bronze sculptures fished up from the sea.

"Gray whales," said Dr. Robert Brownell, the man from Smithsonian.

In a moment the whales surfaced and one after another blew plumes of vapor into the air. Out of the water they lost their lovely green color and turned a dark gray patched with white. The patches, someone said, were barnacles. Cameras clicked and whirred.

"Two pilot whales," said the steadfast Meyerdierks.

We saw the two pilot whales and then three more, and then someone said, "Look at the birds!" in a voice that reminded me of Alfred Hitchcock's movie.

They were off the port bow, a mile away, a flock of birds larger than any I had ever seen—a dark, awesome cloud. It moved toward us and suddenly lowered and fell on the water like a carpet, half a mile in diameter.

"I've never seen anything like it," said Tom Garrison, the professor of oceanography from Orange Coast College.

"How many would you say there are?" I asked Meyer-dierks.

"Between four and five thousand," he said calmly.

No sooner had the birds settled than we saw a pod of sporting porpoises, shooting the waves like boys on surfboards, and then four more gray whales, moving together like submarines attacking in force.

Catalina Island began emerging from the mist. We headed straight for the isthmus to cross to the far side. It was there, the pilot said, that we would find the most gray whales.

The blimp came in low over the isthmus. The cove was leaden under an overcast sky. We floated over the isthmus, looking down on the two harbors. Nothing moved. We might have been a ship from outer space, discovering an abandoned planet.

"Those buildings down there," said Charles Dirks, a professor of political science at L.A. Southwest College, "were union barracks in the Civil War—part of Lincoln's blockade of Confederate spies and smugglers."

We had hardly absorbed this anachronism when another one came. "There's a buffalo down there," someone said.

Like the gray whales we were hunting, the buffalo had once been near extinction. The one we had seen was probably a descendant of a herd abandoned on the island fifty years ago by a Western movie company.

Catalina Harbor, on the far side of the isthmus, looked deserted too. It had been the scene of many hot battles between pirates and sovereign ships, all fought before the cameras for Hollywood.

To eyes used to the cluttered beaches of the mainland, the windward side of Catalina looked as if it might have risen from the ocean floor just yesterday, a bleak granite mountain with sheer cliffs standing like a fortress against wind and sea.

Except for a few gulls, there was no sign of life. The pilot wheeled and descended, chasing shadows in the water. We thought we saw a jellyfish, but it turned out to be a plastic bag—a ubiquitous, proliferating, nonbiodegradable marine pest.

It was late afternoon and the light was fading when the whales began to appear. First a group of five, then a group of four, then six. They were surfacing on all quarters, blowing clouds of vapor, and then flipping up their flukes and sinking out of sight.

They seemed to be moving in random directions, as if enjoying the side trips of their long migration from the Arctic seas to the warm lagoons of Baja California. There they would have their calves and breed and begin the long swim back in the spring.

From the blimp they looked like miniature submarines in the lake on the old back lot at 20th Century–Fox. It was hard to believe they were thirty to fifty feet long and might weigh as much as forty tons, larger in bulk than the largest of the dinosaurs.

Rapacious whalers killed these playful beasts to the edge of extinction in the 1800s and again in the 1930s. But now they are under international protection and coming back. For this respite, they reward us every winter and spring with these leisurely migrations.

One reason they surface, whale watchers believe, is to look around and get their bearings. Evidently they are not driven on their seven-thousand-mile mating voyage by any inner radar or compass. Also, they like to horse around along the way, like American couples traveling in a camper, and have been known to approach boats of awed whale watchers and show off like porpoises in the arenas at Marineland.

It was 5:30, the rush hour, when we flew over the San Diego Freeway on our descent to the Goodyear base. Traffic in the southbound lanes was stop-and-go as the inner city emptied for the day. Low clouds obscured the horizon, and by the tens of thousands the little colored bugs crawled out of the mists and back into the mists again.

We were strangers from outer space, looking down in wonder at these creatures crawling along like colored beads down a thread. What could they be? I couldn't imagine. But whatever they were, they were obviously, quite utterly, stark mad.

SALLY

*"My eyes caught hers. For a moment I thought the old
magic was coming back."*

Feeling crowded by the season, with all its tensions and
obligations, I escaped to the zoo for an hour the other morning
to look at the orangutans.

Of all wild animals I like the orangutan the best. For years
I have kept a portrait of one on my office wall, just above my
typewriter, and I find it very humbling now and then to look
into that curious primate face.

Also, I used to have an affinity with Sally, that earthy
female out at the zoo. I first met her years ago at the old zoo,
where nothing separated us but the screen of her cage. We hit
it off at once, I thought, looking into each other's eyes with an
exciting mutual sense of discovery and recognition; and then
she spit at me. After that our encounters always ended in the
same way.

The morning was cool and misty, a good kind of weather
for the zoo. I walked up the curving road toward the Eurasian
area at the top of the hill, passing the reptile house and Swan
Lake and the aviary. There was a refreshing sound of water
from the lake, and a scarlet macaw scraped my spine with a
shrill cry as I passed her perch.

The first orangutan I saw was a great adult male. He sat
across the moat from me in the lotus position like a yogi wearing a shaggy red rug. He seemed to be in deep meditation. The
eyes were deep-set and dark red; they seemed to lead back,
back into dark caves, one after another, each larger and darker
than the last, and further back in time. What was the brute
thinking about? Perhaps he was searching for that long-forgotten fork in the road where his ancestors had gone one way and
mine the other.

There were three more in the enclosure—two youngsters
and a rather fat adult that I took to be a female. Could it be
Sally? We hadn't seen each other for years. She had been up at

the health center with her declining old mate, Eli, a comfort to him in his sunset days. Now Eli was dead, I'd heard, and Sally was back in circulation.

One of the young ones was sitting at the top of a high tree stump, fighting off the mischievous approaches of the other. The old female was looking at me. I studied her face for signs of emotion. Recognition? Interest? Anything? Nothing. I meant nothing to her. Just another face in the crowd.

An electric cart came up the road with two men in it and one turned out to be Michael Crotty, the zoo's mammal man. Yes, he said, that was Sally. The young female was Sulong, and the young male was Jonathan—both Sally's. The male over there in meditation was Oogie, her new mate. "He's a nice ape," Crotty said.

After Eli died Oogie had been brought in on loan to mate with Sally.

"Did she take to him right away?" I asked.

"Well," Crotty said, "Oogie walked over and gave Sally a push. She pushed him back. He pushed her. She pushed him. He pushed her. Then Sally spit at him and Oogie walked away."

She'll do it every time, I thought.

There were four more orangs in another enclosure up the road. They turned out to be Ahkup, who looked even bigger and meaner than Oogie—a young adult female named Hedda and two more of Sally's children, Gail and Eloise.

"You're a nice girl, Hedda," Crotty said to Hedda. "It's possible she's pregnant," he said to me. "If she is, it would be the first time."

Hedda hadn't been turned on by the first two males she'd been thrown in with. "Poor Hedda," Crotty said. "She's had a rough year. But she likes Ahkup, though by our standards he's the ugliest orang you've ever seen. There's no accounting for taste."

On the way back down the hill I stopped to have another look at Sally. My eyes caught hers. For a moment I thought the old magic was coming back. Then she broke it off. She waddled over to the meditating Oogie and began to groom his neck.

I am not given to the anthropomorphizing of animals. It is not the ways in which they are like us that make them so interesting, but the ways in which they are different. All the same, Sally and I had once known that flash of recognition across the interstellar distance between the species, and now she had forgotten me. Whatever it was that had burned between us, it was now extinguished.

Oh, well, as Crotty had said, there was no accounting for taste.

11

Do You Remember?

PTOMAINE TOMMY'S AND
THE MONTMARTRE

*"Valentino was dating Winifred Hudnut then. Her dog
sat up at the table with them."*

Hoping to draw forth some of the neighborhood history
lying dormant in the memories of longtime Los Angeles residents, I asked a rhetorical question the other day: "Was there
really a Ptomaine Tommy, and did he invent the dish we call
the 'size'?"

As I say, it was rhetorical. I knew there had been a Ptomaine Tommy's out on North Broadway in Lincoln Heights.
Ptomaine Tommy lore had given many vignettes to the late
columnists Gene Sherman and Matt Weinstock. But I wondered how much could be added by Tommy's customers and
friends themselves.

The reports were so many that I can give credit to only a
few, but each helped a bit, piecing in a fact there, a touch of
color there. I heard from many of Tommy's patrons, from an
old girlfriend of his, from his Christian Science practitioner,
and from a onetime beauty operator who used to marcel the
hair of the woman who baked his pies.

Some reports were hazy or erroneous. One said Tommy's
name was Tommy Jacobs; another said it was Tommy Size. It
was really Tommy De Forest, and this is the story:

Tommy had been a law student at some Midwestern university but came to Los Angeles about 1912 and opened a six-
stool lunch wagon that stood in the street on North Broadway

near Avenue 22, directly in front of Madame Rose's Fortune
Telling and Palmist Home.

In World War I he joined the Navy (or was it the Army?).
After the war he came home and started a hamburger and chili
stand a block or so from where the wagon had stood. It prospered. In a few years he opened what was to become the celebrated Ptomaine Tommy's on Broadway near Daly Street.

Tommy's had sawdust on the floor, fresh every day like
the hamburger. The specialty of the house was the size—a
hamburger covered with chili and beans and sprinkled with
chopped onions, called "violets" or "flowers." There were no
booths, at least not at first; just a spotless U-shaped counter,
tended by personable young men in white aprons and chef's
hats. Tommy himself worked behind the counter or at the cash
register by the door. The walls were covered with photographs
of racehorses, prizefighters and celebrities who were regulars
of the place.

Tommy invented the size. The name evolved in this way:
At first he offered his basic dish in two sizes—hamburger size
and steak size. The customer would order the usual. The
waiter would ask, "Which size? Steak size or hamburger size?"
The customer would answer, "Hamburger size," and the
waiter would yell to the kitchen, "Hamburger size!" But few
customers took the steak size, and in time that term was
dropped and the waiter would simply holler "Size!"

"It was a bright, lively place," recalls Lois Seely, whose
grandfather's house was across the street, and Tommy was "a
middle-size, pink-cheeked, pleasant man."

Tommy's was heavily patronized at late hours by neighborhood people from the Starland movie theater up the street,
nurses and interns from the nearby General Hospital, the
after-theater crowd from downtown, and the fight crowd, some
of them in tuxedos and evening dresses.

"My date was an intern," recalls Jean Kennedy of Tujunga.
"We went there at eleven o'clock at night and had to stand
briefly in line. The room was large, airy and spotless."

"I worked as a hairdresser in an arcade next door," writes
Marie Callender of Huntington Beach. "His employees were
all men except one—she was a great pie maker. She was one of
my patrons, and during the week I gave her a reset, that being

the day of the marcel." (One of the problems of dressing the pie cook's hair was the variety of aromas it absorbed at Tommy's.)

Strangely, no one seemed to know or want to say how Ptomaine Tommy's ended. I found this story, not unexpectedly, in the files of the *Times*.

On August 10, 1958, Ptomaine Tommy closed his doors, forced to sell the property to satisfy his creditors. One week later he died. His friends said, of course, it was a broken heart.

Was there really a Montmartre restaurant on Hollywood Boulevard where all the stars ate out and Joan Crawford danced the Charleston?

Yes, indeed, back in the '20s and '30s there was a Montmartre, upstairs in a building just east of Highland, on the north side of the boulevard. Eddie Brandstatter was the owner, and the stars walked upstairs to eat and dance and be seen.

"I proposed to my wife at the Montmartre forty-seven years ago," writes Alex Stept of Palm Springs, "while dancing to the music of the then famous Jackie Taylor orchestra. . . ."

"It is one of my cherished memories of Hollywood," writes Hellen M. Richmond of Santa Monica. "I don't recall ever seeing Joan Crawford doing the Charleston there—but I certainly did it myself. . . ."

"I remember one night in particular," recalls Harley P. Martin, retired Hollywood photographer, "when Jackie Taylor presented a young pianist-composer who had just written an as-yet unpublished song. It was Hoagy Carmichael and his famous 'Stardust.' . . ."

"You may remember me, since you seem to remember many objects of early California," writes Ben Lyon, the engaging star who played in eighty movies. "Married Bebe Daniels, and in 1936 went to London for a three-week engagement with her at the London Palladium and remained in that marvelous city for thirty-six years. (Dear Bebe passed away in 1971.)

"I have before me a Montmartre table card announcement which calls your attention to the Halloween Carnival Special night, Saturday the 29th, 1927. It suggests making your reservations early. There will be dancing and favors and a dancing contest for a surprise trophy.

"I used the announcement card to send a message to a

beautiful girl—Marion Nixon, then a Universal star. I asked her if she would join me for 'a large cup of demitasse.' She did and I was thrilled meeting her. Forty-seven years later she became my wife. . . ."

"I visited Southern California in the winter of 1922," writes Irene Leache of Laguna Hills, "staying a week with my friend Dolly Gosiger, who was the cashier at the Montmartre. It was the time of the tea dansant and they danced at lunchtime too. Often the waiter would point out celebrities to me . . . Valentino was dating Winifred Hudnut then. Her dog sat up at the table with them. . . ."

"I can close my eyes now," writes Lita Grey Chaplin, who was then the wife of Charlie Chaplin, "and still see vividly the scene before me . . . Joan Crawford and Hedda Hopper, my luncheon companions, seated with me at a small, round window table. Joan with her freckled complexion and huge eyes. Hedda with the finely chiseled features of a sculptor's choice for beauty. The room alive with the sounds of a packed restaurant —loud talk, laughter and the New York beat of the dance band. . . ."

"I was there one evening in June, 1921," recalls George H. Stitzel, "when the highlight was listening to a vocal trio singing 'Bye Bye Blackbird.' . . . their names were Al Rinker, Harry Barris and Bing Crosby. . . ."

But did Joan Crawford do the Charleston there? "I was there when she did it, one Friday night in 1924, I think," recalls Robert Lawrence Balzer, the distinguished food and wine writer. Balzer was only "a precocious twelve years old" at the time, but he and his girlfriend, Mary Archambault, had brazened their way into the Montmartre "to hit the big-time dance contest circuit."

"The room was star-studded. Joan Crawford was there with Tommy Lee, the playboy son of Cadillac dealer Don Lee. Ricardo Cortez danced every dance, including the contest, with Alma Rubens. . . . That we won the contest seems altogether too unreal. But it did happen at the Montmartre. . . ."

Finally, a word from Miss Crawford herself, quoted by Kathleen M. Orvis of Santa Monica, from the autobiography *A Portrait of Joan.*

"And I loved to dance. At the Montmartre overlooking

Hollywood Boulevard, the gayest people lunched, dined and supper-clubbed while tourists were held back by red velvet ropes. . . . I worked all day, danced all night. . . ."

All things considered, I think I would have preferred the Montmartre to Ptomaine Tommy's.

THE GREAT AIR RAID

"A warden named Campbell fell down his own front
stairs and broke his arm."

"I've been reading *The Glory and the Dream* by William Manchester," writes Carol Cecchini of Glendale, "and on page 323 he says, 'Jap submarines shelled Seattle, and fifteen carrier-borne Zeros bombed Los Angeles in early March.'

"Do you remember this really happening? I would be interested in knowing if Manchester has his facts right."

I am grateful to Mrs. Cecchini for giving me an excuse for reviewing the facts of what was certainly among the most wonderful diversions of World War II—the Great Los Angeles Air Raid.

First, I looked into Manchester's book myself to make sure that Mrs. Cecchini had quoted him correctly. She had. Manchester even goes on to add his own personal appraisal of the actions he described: "Militarily," he says, "the attacks were only of nuisance value, but as psychological thrusts they were brilliant."

Actually, the Great Los Angeles Air Raid did not occur in March but on the night of February 25, 1942. It began at 2:25 A.M. when the U.S. Army announced the approach of hostile aircraft and the city's air-raid warning system went into effect for the first time in World War II.

Suddenly the night was rent by sirens. Searchlights began to sweep the sky. Minutes later gun crews at Army forts along the coastline began pumping the first of 1,433 rounds of ack-ack into the moonlight.

Thousands of volunteer air-raid wardens tumbled from their beds and grabbed their boots and helmets. Citizens awakened to the screech of sirens and, heedless of the blackout warning, began snapping on their lights. Policemen turned to. Reporters rushed into the streets.

The din continued unabated for two hours. Finally the guns fell silent. The enemy, evidently, had been routed. Los Angeles began to taste the exhilaration of its first military victory.

The *Times* was on the streets at daylight with a dramatic account of that gaudy night: "Roaring out of a brilliant moonlit western sky, foreign aircraft flying both in large formation and singly flew over Southern California early today and drew heavy barrages of antiaircraft fire—the first ever to sound over United States continental soil against an enemy invader."

But the second paragraph was rather a letdown: "No bombs were reported dropped."

However, the account went on, "At 5 A.M. the police reported that an airplane had been shot down near 185th Street and Vermont Avenue. Details were not available. . . ." (Neither, as it turned out later, was the airplane.)

Though no bombs had been dropped, the city had not escaped its baptism of fire without casualties, including five fatalities. So many cars were dashing back and forth in the blackout that three persons were killed in automobile collisions. Two others died of heart attacks.

A radio announcer named Stokey, hurrying to get to his post in the dark, suffered a deep laceration over his right eye when he ran into an awning. A policeman named Larker, seeing a light on in a Hollywood store, kicked in the window and suffered a half-inch laceration on his right leg. A *Times* reporter, hurrying from his Inglewood home to the nearby police station, underestimated the height of a curbing and jolted his backbone.

The toll was particularly high among air-raid wardens, who were said to have acted with valor throughout. In Pasadena a warden named Hoffman fell from a five-foot wall while looking into a lighted apartment and fractured a leg. Another named Barber jumped a three-foot fence in Hollywood to reach a house that had a light on and sprained his right ankle. A warden named Campbell fell down his own front stairs and broke his left arm.

There was also scattered structural damage. Several roofs were holed by ack-ack projectiles that had failed to explode in the sky but worked fine as soon as they struck ground, demolishing a room here, a patio there, and in one case blowing out the tire of a parked automobile.

Exultation turned to outrage the next day when the Secretary of the Navy said there had been no enemy planes at all. It was just a case of "jitters." The Army, being thus accused of shooting up an empty sky, was outraged. Los Angeles authorities were outraged, especially the sheriff, who had valiantly helped the FBI round up numerous Japanese nurserymen and gardeners who were supposedly caught in the act of signaling the enemy planes.

At length the Secretary of War came up with a face-saving theory. There had been no enemy military planes, but it was believed there had been fifteen "commercial" planes flown by "enemy agents." Though no one believed this romantic fancy, most agreed with the Secretary of War that "It is better to be too alert than not alert enough."

No, Mrs. Cecchini, Manchester doesn't have his facts right. There was no aircraft carrier. There were no Zeros. There were no bombs. There was no raid.

The Great Los Angeles Air Raid may have been nothing more than a great piece of slapstick, but many residents still have vivid memories of that night on which the city fought so valiantly against the enemy who wasn't there.

Among those who have written to set the record straight is my friend and colleague Don Dwiggins, onetime aviation editor of the Los Angeles *Daily News.*

"I was there," Dwiggins writes, "and well remember all the shooting at the UFOs. . . . As you recall, people 'saw' all sorts of things, but the USAF report concludes: 'A careful study of the evidence suggests that meteorological balloons—known to have been released over Los Angeles—may well have caused the initial alarm.' "

Raid or no raid, the night was not without its moments of real drama.

"I will never forget that night," writes Jean Ballantyne of Pasadena, "because I was in Hollywood Presbyterian Hospital having my first child. All the new mothers felt as helpless as I did amid all the sirens and searchlights, so in the pitch-black halls the nurses came along handing out babies to anxious mothers. I will never know to this day if I had the right one, but it doesn't matter. Wasn't that a humane and thoughtful thing for the maternity nurses to do?"

Martha Griffin, now a retired nurse, was working the night shift at County Hospital when the first alert came and had to help black out the windows.

"It was not all that simple, as the small transom windows on top had no shades and had not been open for years. We were supplied with dark gray blankets with which to cover these small windows. Ladders were provided and we were told great caution should be taken. And who was doing the hanging? The nurses. And who was helping? The ambulatory patients—with oral help from the bed patients. We were given candles to use on our medicine charts and at our desks in the center hall.

"But, Jack, I think fear in some instances brings people closer than joy. My observations that night confirmed this. The patients' complaints were fewer and also their demands. Amazingly enough they asked for fewer sleeping capsules! Do you think they wanted to be awake to see what it was all about? It took two weeks to have all the hundreds of windows painted black. Years later they were scraped clean again to let in the light. And so it goes."

R. H. Pearsall of Arcadia was an air-raid warden and points out that not very many wardens could have "grabbed their boots and helmets," as I wrote. "In most of Los Angeles helmets had not yet been issued.

"About a block from my house an ack-ack battery had been set up across from the phone building near Vernon and Western," he recalls. "As I scanned the sky I could see the bursts from this battery, illuminated by the searchlights, but nothing else. Frankly, I was very skeptical of the whole thing."

I think I can safely lay the Great Air Raid to rest with a report from another friend and colleague, Marvin Miles, our aviation expert.

"As a survivor of both the Great Air Raid and the dangers of penetrating the blackout to reach the *Times* city room that night," he says in a memo, "may I call your attention to Volume One of the *Army Air Forces in World War II,* which devotes some three pages to the incident in which 1,400 rounds of antiaircraft ammunition were expended, no bombs dropped and no planes shot down.

"In sum, the history points out (1) that the Japanese at war's end said they sent no planes over the area, (2) that much of the confusion came from shellbursts caught by searchlight beams which themselves were mistaken for enemy planes, and (3) that 'a careful study of the evidence suggests that meteorological balloons, known to have been released over Los Angeles, may well have caused the initial alarm—a theory supported by the fact that antiaircraft artillery units were officially criticized for having wasted ammunition on targets which moved too slowly to have been airplanes.'

"The weather [wind] balloons, as I recall from my own study of the event," Miles concludes, "were released in connection with the operation of barrage balloons. At night the small balloons carried lights for tracking purposes and the presumption was that someone goofed and forgot to inform control points that a balloon was being released. Hence the flying light, the first antiaircraft shot and then the fusillade."

I guess that ought to hold the people who say Los Angeles has no history.

As for William Manchester's error, he has explained it himself in a gracious note, as follows:

"A friend has sent me a copy of your column, and I blush to admit that you're right on target: I *didn't* have my fact right in that instance.

"Actually I've received several letters from California chastising me. And I've mended my ways. My only excuse for slipping in the first case was that the nonexistent raid was reported in the *New York Times,* and as a vassal of the Eastern Establishment press, I accepted the *Times* account as gospel.

"In any event, the blunder has been corrected in the second edition. . . .

"Clearly in this instance I would have been wiser to consult the *Los Angeles Times.*"

It was a glorious night.

12
Men of Science

THE RICHTER SCALE

"It fractured rails and melons,/It fractured female felons. . . ."

Years ago, when I was a reporter working at the whim of the city editor, I was sent to Caltech to cover a seminar in a field of mathematics so abstruse that they said it couldn't be described in English, much less explained.

I had the vain notion that anything could be described in English and that if it could be described in English I could understand it. My mission was a failure. The subject wasn't far out, either, like the curvature of space and time. It had to do with such everyday things as wallpaper patterns. But that's as far as I got.

So I was gratified the other day when I stumbled onto a Caltech project that I do understand. It has engaged some of the institute's finest minds and talents for two decades, and now their work has been encapsulated in a phonograph record called "Let's Advance on Science," which is in plain English.

"Let's Advance on Science" is a patchwork of pieces from an open-ended musical comedy that has been twenty years in production by Kent Clark, professor of English, and Elliott Davis, who is said to have worked his way through Syracuse playing banjo and jazz piano. Occasionally, through the years, their work in progress has been performed, or perhaps one should say executed, for Caltech audiences, by Clark, Davis and the Caltech Stock Company, which is to music what the Caltech football team is to sports.

The record was put together from tapes of live shows and is a bit ragged, but it is rendered no less charming by miscues, flats, ellipses, wandering counterpoints, malapropisms and Freudian slips. The music is catchy and the lyrics are as good as anything understandable that has come out of Caltech since Dr. Millikan's dissertation on cosmic rays.

Some of the songs of course are inside jokes, but anyone who has lived in Los Angeles very long can enjoy "The Richter Scale," which begins:

Charley Richter made a scale for calibrating earthquakes
Gives a true and lucid reading every time the earth
*   shakes*
Increments are exponential, numbers 0 to nine
When the first shock hit the seismo everything worked
*   fine*
It measured
One two on the Richter scale, a shabby little shiver
One two on the Richter scale, a queasy little quiver. . . .

The song goes on through the Long Beach quake:

Nineteen hundred thirty-three and Long Beach rocked
*   and rumbled*
Schoolhouse walls and crockery and oil derricks
*   tumbled*
Hollywood got hit but good, it even shook the stars
Shattered glass and spilled martinis on a hundred bars,
*   it measured*
Six three on the Richter scale. . . .

Then the Tehachapi quake:

Came the turn of County Kern, the mountains lurched
*   and trembled*
Bakersfield, which jerked and reeled, was almost
*   disassembled. . . .*
It measured
Seven eight on the Richter scale, it fractured rails and
*   melons*
Seven eight on the Richter scale, it fractured female
*   felons*

Next, the Alaska quake:

Eight five on the Richter scale, it loosened kelp and
*   corals*

*Eight five on the Richter scale, it loosened faith and
  morals. . . .*

And finally the big one that is yet to come:

*Some day pretty soon we fear our many faults will fail
  us
Slide and slip and rip and dip and all at once assail us
Seismic jolts like lightning bolts will flatten us that day
When the concrete settles down geologists will say it
  measured
Eight nine on the Richter scale. . . .*

As much fun as earthquakes can be, though, my favorite
of the Kent Clark songs is "A Nice Girl Like You," in which
the boys, bemused by the admission of women students to
Caltech, ask the question:

*What's a nice girl like you doing in a place like this?
A nice girl like you should be doing something better
A nice girl like you ought to be as free as air
Waving at a star now, cruising in a car now
Strumming a guitar now, laughing in a bar now
Something light and easy, something bright and breezy
Pleasing a lovely miss
Never in a place like this. . . .*

And the girl answers:

*What's a nice girl like me doing in a place like this?
A nice girl like me happens to be fond of physics
A nice girl like me wants to be an engineer
Fond of mathematics, fond of hydrostatics
Any new dimension, any new invention
Wild about a photon, gamma ray or proton,
No ton I want to miss
Being in a place like this. . . .*

Maybe Kent Clark won't win a Nobel Prize for musical
comedy, or even for peace, but it's comforting to know that
they're doing something there at Caltech besides talking in
tongues about wallpaper.

EINSTEIN IN THE WILDERNESS

"There was Einstein . . . arguing with a barrel cactus."

By an occurrence of serendipity, for which I seem to have a gift, I went out to Caltech the other day to see a scientist, his specialty being a field I am unable to explain. He wasn't in. But in wandering around the campus I ran into Judith Goodstein, Caltech's archivist.

A year or two ago Goodstein undertook the job of putting Caltech's archives together. There is some truth, I think, in the legend that people of scientific genius are inept in the everyday business of keeping their houses in order. So are the rest of us, but in an ordinary person ineptness isn't regarded as unordinary.

When Goodstein was employed, she was led down into the basement of the new library building, a monument to the sainted Dr. Robert Millikan. The building, by the way, is tall and modern, unlike the rest of Caltech's structures, and is known to the students as Millikan Federal Savings. Anyway that's the last I heard. I can't expect to keep up with what Caltech students are thinking.

What Goodstein found was a litter of priceless letters, memorandums, doodlings and documents by the best minds of the century, so far. Also there were typically banal letters from United States Presidents, from the first Roosevelt up to Richard Nixon; some of them, certainly Teddy's, had been written by the Presidents themselves. But there were also little scraps of gossip and chatty exchanges between people like Einstein, Millikan, and Richard Tolman.

Amid this treasure Goodstein found a trivial document which she said I was free to use. It has never been published, but I think it ought to be, because it suggests that scientists are human. It is simply a few words Tolman spoke at a banquet in Einstein's honor. Beyond that I think it needs no explanation. It follows:

"Fellow scientists, I should like to explain to you the reason why I happen to be toastmaster this evening. Three weeks ago in the late afternoon I was strolling back and forth on the institute campus, buried in meditation, trying to find a solution for the terrible problem of the increase in entropy that appears to be taking place everywhere throughout the universe. Just at that moment when it seemed as if I were about to get a solution to the problem, my walk was suddenly interrupted by Dr. Millikan.

" 'Tolman,' he said. Dr. Millikan is an older man than I am and he always speaks to me in that informal way . . . but I always reply, 'Yes, sir—yes, Dr. Millikan.'

" 'Tolman,' he said, 'I think it would be a good plan if we had a dinner at which the members of the scientific staff and neighboring institutions could meet with Dr. Professor Einstein.'

" 'Dr. Millikan,' I replied, 'I think that would be very fine for the staff members but pretty hard on Professor Einstein. I am sure he has had to attend so many dinners in his honor that he never wants to look another filet mignon in the face. I therefore recommend strongly against such a dinner.'

"Two weeks ago today I was again strolling back and forth on the campus and had again nearly reached the solution of the problem of entropy and was again interrupted by Dr. Millikan. 'Tolman,' he said, 'I have been thinking about your suggestion that we ought to have a staff dinner in honor of Dr. Einstein, and I believe we ought to have a number of speeches by staff members.' 'Dr. Millikan,' I said, 'I recommend strongly against any speeches.'

"One week ago today I was again strolling back and forth on the campus and had again nearly reached the solution to the problem of entropy and was again interrupted by Dr. Millikan. 'Tolman,' he said, 'I have been thinking about your suggestion that we ought to have speeches at the dinner for Dr. Einstein. Here is the list of speakers. Also, I have decided to appoint you to be the toastmaster.'

"That, fellow scientists, is the reason why I am the toastmaster tonight and the reason why the problem of entropy remains unresolved.

"But now, gentlemen, I have a surprising and wonderful piece of good news for you. On Saturday morning a meeting was held . . . by the proposed speakers. With great good sense and judgment, that body of speakers decided the dinner would be more enjoyable for Professor Einstein if they didn't speak. That, gentlemen, was the most intelligent group of men ever gathered together within four walls."

Ironically, it was Dr. Millikan himself, the author of Tolman's ordeal, who once walked out of an interminable service-club dinner at which he was to be the speaker, saying, "Gentlemen, it is my bedtime."

As for entropy, I don't know. I looked it up in the dictionary and I still don't know. But Dr. Tolman, in striking such a blow against banquets and dinner speeches, has paid humanity a much greater service than the scientist who may someday solve the problem of entropy, whatever it is.

Later I drove to Caltech in the rain one morning to call on Goodstein and talk of her favorite subject again. My visit was in answer to a letter she had written weeks earlier, asking if I would help her beat the bushes for stories or photographs that might help her in preparing a paper on Albert Einstein in Southern California.

"For instance, I recently learned that he paid a visit (in 1931 or '32 or '33) to a Beaumont hotel . . . whose owners encouraged their guests to go horseback riding. I would give my kingdom for a picture of Einstein on a horse. Does anyone have such a snapshot tucked away in a long-forgotten scrapbook?"

I found Goodstein in her basement office, sitting in the late Dr. Millikan's chair, at Millikan's desk. She showed me through vaults of orderly files that she and her staff had created out of a chaos of precious memorabilia cast off by generations of absent-minded geniuses. From one box came dozens of letters in the minuscule German hand of Einstein himself.

Goodstein put on a sweater and a woolly cap and we walked in the rain to the Athenaeum for lunch. Einstein and his wife Elsa had been lodged in the Athenaeum, and often he sat in its classic dining room with Dr. Millikan and other colleagues. In fact, the sainted Dr. Millikan looked down at us from an oil painting on the wall.

In return for my help in finding a snapshot of Einstein on a horse, or its like, Goodstein had promised to give me an

Einstein story, noting that several rare ones had been turned up recently in oral-history interviews with retired Caltech professors. She had picked one told by Winchester (Winch) Jones, professor emeritus of English, about a motor trip he had taken to the desert nearly fifty years ago with Einstein, the physicist Paul (Eppy) Epstein and one or two other deep thinkers.

"I was driving," Jones recalled, "because none of the rest of them had driven sand roads before. You can't see the desert unless you get off into the canyons. And I knew one place that might prove good. . . . We got to the end of the paving and started out on the sand road . . . and let most of the air out of the tires, so you don't skitter off, you stay in the ruts.

"We drove six or seven miles up this canyon, a beautiful canyon, a lot of typical desert flora and views and rocks, and Einstein was quite impressed with the whole thing. So we had lunch and some discussion started that was way beyond me. It had to do with the red shift. I still don't know what the red shift is.

"Finally, I thought, boy, we better get started back . . . get back on the paving before dark. And so back we went . . . and I said, 'All right, boys, get out and pump up the tires.' So everybody got out. Well, there had been a tremendous argument going on in the back seat on this same subject—the red shift —all in German. I hadn't understood a word of it. I had concentrated the whole time on keeping in those ruts. So I looked around and by golly Einstein wasn't there. He simply wasn't there. I said, 'Where in the world is Einstein?' 'Einstein? Oh, we must have left him.'

"Well, I was scared to death. I said, 'We've killed our greatest scientist. He'll die of thirst up there.' So back we went. As fast as I could drive. And there was Einstein, happy as a clam. He was arguing with a barrel cactus. Now a barrel cactus looks very much like Paul Epstein . . . and *Einstein* was nearsighted.

" 'Oh, Jones," he says, 'are we going? At last I have convinced Eppy on the red shift. For half an hour he says nothing.' "

Being skeptical, Goodstein asked Alice Epstein, Paul's widow, if she remembered the incident. No, she hadn't gone along on the trip. But she said, "If *Paul* had been driving, it certainly could have happened."

We walked back to the basement and Goodstein showed me a paper she had read in Rome on Einstein and the great Italian mathematician Tullio Levi-Civita, with whom he had engaged for years, by letter, in a friendly but dogged argument over "the nature of the external world."

"Look at the last line," Goodstein said.

I read it: "The story is told that Einstein, when asked what he best liked about Italy, replied, 'Spaghetti and Levi-Civita.' "

"It might just be true," she said.

13

The Way They Were

THE LANA TURNER STORY

"I was not discovered at Schwab's drugstore."

It's been some years since I carried a press card, but I did some investigative reporting into a Hollywood myth the other day, and I found out I haven't lost the old know-how. Maybe, like every other reporter in America, I was fired up by the dogged work of Redford and Hoffman in *All the President's Men.*

I had just heard from two former colleagues, both of them questioning something I had written about the legend that Lana Turner was discovered while sitting at the soda fountain of Schwab's drugstore on Sunset Boulevard. It's a story, myth or not, that doesn't die. It is Holy Writ, as sacred as Adam and Eve.

Ironically, I was not telling the story myself this time, but merely commenting on an article about Los Angeles by Jan Morris, the English writer, in *Rolling Stone* magazine. She had written that Miss Turner was discovered while "sitting on a bar stool" in Schwab's. I had corrected her, noting that Miss Turner had not been sitting on a bar stool but at the soda fountain, having an ice-cream soda.

One letter came from Bill Kennedy, who used to sit next to me on the rewrite desk at the old *Herald-Express.* "You wrote that Lana Turner was discovered while sipping a soda at Schwab's drugstore," he said. "I always heard that it was the drugstore across from Hollywood High School at Sunset and Highland. The store is now a gas station, I believe.

"Anyway, the Universal Studios research library, which is supposed to know about such cataclysmic events, reports that

. . . Lana was discovered in January, 1936, by Billy Wilkerson, founder of the *Hollywood Reporter*, while she was sipping a Coke at a drugstore. Doesn't say which drugstore. Now, why don't you get Lana on the phone and settle this momentous question for all time? Millions of shopgirls everywhere are waiting."

The other came from Donovan Roberts, another of the old gang at the *Herald-Express*. "Certainly," he said, "we know that this great event did not take place at Schwab's, and anyway, the present Schwab's is not the Schwab's of Lana's discovery date.

"But you and Ms. Morris both miss the important point. Just where was the soda fountain? My recollection of the Hollywood folk tale is that the soda fountain was situated on Highland Avenue across from Hollywood High. . . .

"Isn't it time that something concrete should be done about this? Has anyone ever asked Lana Turner about the details? . . . It is time to get this historic moment in Los Angeles history related accurately, and since you failed to recognize the need in your offhand correction of the Jan Morris error, it seems to me that you should take the lead."

I decided to accept the challenge. Where to begin? First I called my friend Jet Fore, head press agent at 20th Century–Fox. I have always thought that Fore knows everything about Hollywood, and if he doesn't he knows who does. I asked him about the Lana Turner story.

"I don't believe it," he said. "I think some press agent made it up, the way I made up the one about how Marilyn Monroe was discovered."

"What was that?"

"She was baby-sitting. The guy just happened to be a casting director. The regular baby-sitter had to go home and got Marilyn to take her place. When the guy got home and saw Marilyn he said, 'Hey, you oughta be in pitchers!' "

"You made that up?"

"Jack," he said, "have I ever lied to you?"

I decided to phone Tichi Wilkerson Miles, publisher of the *Hollywood Reporter*. She had been Billy Wilkerson's wife and might have heard him tell the story. I phoned, but she wasn't in.

I decided to ask Charles Champlin, our movie critic. I

walked over to his office, but he was on the phone and had someone waiting.

By sheer luck I happened to be waiting for an elevator when Phil Scheuer stepped out of one. Phil had been our young movie critic when Lana was discovered. He said Mervyn LeRoy would know. I phoned LeRoy and he remembered the name of the casting director but not which drugstore.

I thought of calling Miss Turner herself, but decided against it. I didn't know her number for one thing, and anyway she probably wasn't home. Besides, it was bad form to go directly to the principal. Redford and Hoffman never phoned Dick Nixon, did they?

At the moment I'm willing to compromise. Lana Turner was discovered in the drugstore across the street from Hollywood High, not at Schwab's. But she was having an ice-cream soda, not a Coke. Of that I feel quite sure.

And unless I'm very much mistaken, it was vanilla.

Any man of my vintage, or any vintage for that matter, can understand the thrill I felt when I picked up my telephone messages and found that Lana Turner had called me and left her number.

Evidently word had got to her that I was investigating the story of her discovery back in 1936, and she was ready to talk. At last, I realized, I might be able to rescue the truth from the haze and error in which it had become enveloped.

The truth had not been easy to discover under the layers of time and legend. Some of the principals had passed from the scene. Others were themselves victims of the mythologizing of Hollywood, where tiny facts are enclosed and obscured in opalescent fantasies, as grains of sand are enclosed in pearls. Phones went unanswered. Memories proved blank or faulty. Faith had given way to cynicism.

I dialed Miss Turner's number. Someone answered. I gave my name and she came to the phone. Here is her story:

"This will be," she said, "the five thousand five hundredth time I have told the true story, and yet I am still asked the question, over and over again, to the point where I say to myself—dear Lord!—I'm not getting through to people! But nobody listens.

"The true story is, I was *not* discovered at Schwab's drugstore sitting on a stool. In fact, I wish I had *stock* in Schwab's. They've lived off me for over thirty years now. I've been told about these young girls, they hit the Hollywood trail, and they go and sit on these stools at Schwab's and nothing happens, because that isn't where it happened!

"Now here is where and how it happened. I was going to Hollywood High and I cut a typing class, because it was boring and I guess I had no plans to become a secretary anyway. And I went across Sunset Boulevard and there was this little malt shop. I was sitting there and the place was totally empty, because all the good students were doing what they were supposed to do."

"What flavor was your ice-cream soda?" I asked. "It's important."

"I believe they had strawberry sodas, chocolate sodas—I do not truthfully remember, but I do remember that it could only have cost a nickel, because that's how poor we were. It was probably a Coca-Cola.

"They had a counter like a square horseshoe kind of thing, and this gentleman, way over on the other side, I noticed was looking at me. I lowered my eyes. I mean you know, I wasn't *that* green."

The gentleman spoke to the proprietor. The proprietor spoke to Julie (not yet Lana), whom he knew as a regular customer. He said the gentleman was a legitimate gentleman and wanted to be introduced.

"So I said, 'All right, but you stay right by me.' He, the gentleman, turned out to be Mr. Billy Wilkerson, of the *Hollywood Reporter*. He looked at me and said, 'How would you like to be in the movies?' And I looked right back at him and said, 'I don't know—I'll have to ask my mother.' And that is the God's truth!"

The rest of the story, of course, is history. Miss Turner did ask her mother and went on to become a star and to demonstrate, in *The Postman Always Rings Twice*, among other films, that she could project more sex in a white frock than most of today's stars can in the buff.

I don't expect to win the Pulitzer Prize for this. I suspect the awards committee loads the dice in favor of political reporting, anyway. But I hope I never see again, in print, the canard that Lana Turner was discovered in Schwab's drugstore.

I'd still prefer to think she was having a vanilla ice-cream soda. But I'll have to accept Miss Turner's recollection that it was a Coke. After all, it was her nickel.

NELLIE DURFEE

"Nellie fell in love with her mother's dashing driver."

By now the furnishings and the personal belongings of Nellie Durfee will have been removed from her Tudor mansion on West Adams Boulevard, and the rooms in which she had lived in widowhood for the past fifty years, almost unvisited by outsiders, will be bare.

A week or two ago it was my good luck, through the courtesy of Robert Hanson, a fellow governor of the Calcutta Saddle and Cycle Club, to look inside the house, before it was stripped by the auctioneers, and into the life of Mrs. Durfee. Hanson is an officer of the Title Insurance & Trust Company, which is handling the Durfee estate, and he gave me a tour, along with his English colleague Vincent Shepherd.

In the pretentious past the city's first millionaires built their ornate domiciles along West Adams to show off their wealth and refinement and to isolate themselves from the grubby sources of their fortunes. One by one, up and down the boulevard, the palaces have been dismantled or taken over by charitable foundations and modernized; but Mrs. Durfee had held out against this encroachment on her life-style.

She lived in seclusion, in semi-mourning, in an eternal 1926. She kept her house in the past, hidden from the changing world by aged trees. Just six months short of her hundredth birthday, wasted and blind, she died at last in her upstairs bedroom alone with her companion-housekeeper, her cat, her ostrich feathers, her unopened boxes of silk stockings, her sculptures and paintings and her Oriental rugs.

She left more than a million dollars besides the house and all it held, but there were no close relatives. There was a will, but in some details it was out of date: She had outlived its beneficiaries. Still, there were valid bequests: "The cat got in," I was told, "for seventeen thousand dollars."

A clue to Nellie Durfee's attitude toward heirs might be drawn from a cartoon she had cut out and kept. It showed a lawyer reading a will to a group of glum-looking heirs: ". . . and so, being of sound mind, I spent every last damn cent I had. . . ."

We unlocked a wrought-iron gate on a side street and drove into Mrs. Durfee's grounds—three acres of lawns, orchards, arbors, hedges and great old trees, unrestrained by the pruner's shears. Nymphs and cupids grinned at us as we walked up to the door to be let in by Eva Neumann, the housekeeper. She had been Mrs. Durfee's eyes and companion for the last twelve years of her life.

The entrance hall might have been the showroom of a Persian rug merchant. Dark blue, wine red, beige, green and ocher, the rugs lay across the polished floors and climbed the cedar stairways. Mrs. Durfee had loved Oriental rugs; there were seventy of them in the house.

She also loved stained-glass windows, bronze and marble sculptures, and oil paintings, especially her own. She had tried her hand at various decorative crafts and had painted prolifically, in the manner of a tutored Grandma Moses, until the blindness of her last decade.

Miss Neumann led us into the garden drawing room. Bronze and marble nymphs, beasts, birds and children. Seventeenth-century chairs, brass Chinese urns, Art Nouveau lighting fixtures, a Kirman carpet . . . It was a room in which, for half a century, Mrs. Durfee had received few callers—perhaps a deferential nephew, a hopeful ecclesiastic from the church-owned property next door, a solicitous lawyer or physician. But mostly the lady of the house had stayed upstairs with her paints and brushes, or in her bed, or out on the porch in the sun, being read to by Miss Neumann.

Helen (Nellie) Belle McGaughey was born in Chattanooga on July 11, 1876, and as an infant had come to Los Angeles with her wealthy mother, Elizabeth Gates McGaughey, who soon married an immigrant Italian laundryman named Nick Bonfilio. Mrs. Bonfilio became the foremost woman breeder of harness racing horses in Los Angeles, and her husband became a banker and substantial citizen.

Mrs. Bonfilio's fame as a horsewoman was much bur-

nished, evidently, by the skill of William George Durfee, a
driver who carried her colors. Indeed, Mrs. Bonfilio thought so
highly of young Durfee that she was quoted in the *Times* as
saying that she would rather lose any horse in her stable than
lose his services.

It is not surprising that Nellie fell in love with her
mother's dashing driver, even though he already had a wife.
That obstacle, however, was soon removed, as reported in a
Santa Barbara newspaper:

> ### PLUNGER LEFT,
> ### LOVED ANOTHER WOMAN
> SANTA MONICA—*Jennie Durfee, a handsome, well-
> groomed woman, was plaintiff in a divorce suit in Judge
> Cole's court yesterday, and she got her decree. W. G. Dur-
> fee, a well-known horseman, was the defendant, and the
> charge was desertion. Durfee has made his home in this
> city between seasons, and he is known as one of the big
> plungers.*
>
> *The Durfees were married in 1897, and in 1907 the
> wife became suspicious of his loyalty to her. She received
> a tip that hubby was in San Francisco lingering with an
> unknown woman, and she went north herself to see if the
> reports were true. They were. . . .*

Perhaps Mrs. Bonfilio did not think her prize driver quite
so suitable as a son-in-law, even if her daughter was already
thirty-five. In any case, if Mrs. Bonfilio also was an obstacle,
death conveniently removed her on June 5, 1911, and four
months later Nellie married Durfee.

For a time they lived in a house at 21st and Figueroa
streets, using it as a base for their continual honeymoons
abroad, but in 1920 it was sold and torn down for a Pierce-
Arrow factory, and the Durfees bought the house on Adams.

"When I came here," said Miss Neumann as she led us up
a stairway to the bedrooms, "she was living on crackers and
milk."

At last we stood in Durfee's bedroom, which his widow
had locked away from all but her own eyes for half a century.
It was 1926. That had been a vintage year: Ernest Hemingway
published *The Sun Also Rises*. Bobby Jones won the U.S. Open.
Gertrude Ederle swam the English Channel. A man named

Buzzacchino invented the permanent wave. And Calvin Coolidge sat complacently in the White House, allowing all those wonderful things to happen.

William Durfee had been a gentleman of his times, a Great Gatsby who got the girl. His traveling cases were of genuine cowhide, plastered over with the stickers of Europe's finest resorts. His felt hats, wide-brimmed and luxuriant, bore the label of Alexander & Oviatt, the gentleman's store on Olive Street. His suits and coats were of excellent worsted and tweed. Silver cups, photographs and clippings attested to his prowess on the track. I wondered if his ghost had ever escaped this room.

The only other sign of Durfee's presence in his house was the billiard table in the ballroom on the third floor. It was a narrow room, squeezed in under the main gable of the Tudor-style house, but nearly a hundred feet long. The long, long walls were a gallery of Mrs. Durfee's own paintings—dozens of them. And at the far end from the billiard table sat her Steinway grand.

I lifted the piano bench lid and found some sheet music and a few crumbling clippings from the *Times*. One of them, dated March 3, 1915, was a report, out of Constantinople, that the British cruiser *Zephyr* had been badly damaged in an attack on the Dardanelles and had withdrawn to Salonika with one hundred fifty wounded. Another, dated October 4, 1924, was an interview with a "specialist" who warned women against bobbing their hair. "As a woman grows mannish in appearance," he prophesied, "she will grow mannish in nature. This is the inevitable psychological consequence."

If the news was grim, there was music to restore the spirit. "The Always Joyful Gallop" was there and "The First Kiss Waltz" and the top hit of 1926, "When Day Is Done."

I had a hunch that when his day was done William Durfee went below to his cellar in search of something more vivifying. The three of us did the same.

It was a treasure. Shelves of sherry, Scotch, bourbon, rum, gin and brandy; cases of Bordeaux, cognac and champagne. And none of it had been touched for fifty years. The labels were enough to make a wine buff weep: Pontet Canet, 1905, Bordeaux; Chateau Lafite, 1903; Chateau Mouton-Rothschild,

1896. And the whiskies, the famous whiskies! Old Bushmills, Three Feathers, Brook Hill sour mash, Old Crow, Crab Orchard, Old Overholt, Three Rivers, Four Roses, Old Charter, Haig Glenleven and pinchbottle Haig & Haig: 183 bottles of whisky, and not to mention port, marsala, triple sec, creme de cacao, chartreuse and gallons of California wine in bulk. All this stowed away in the very depths of Prohibition! Whatever William Durfee's failings as a husband, he had certainly been a good provider.

I would have given the Rams' No. 2 draft choice to pull a cork—let us say a bottle of Chateau Yquem and Bordeaux, not to be greedy—but, alas, the whole lot was to be sold at auction by Sotheby Parke Bernet.

Mrs. Durfee evidently thought she had her husband's ghost locked up tight in his closet. But I wouldn't be surprised if Durfee's spirit was down in his cellar, instead, and when its new owner draws his first cork, perhaps from a bottle of Chateau Mouton-Rothschild, 1896, William Durfee will come out.

THE RETURN OF JOHN McKAY

"He looked like some exotic white-crested
Florida cockatoo."

We went to the Coliseum last Saturday evening to see The Return of John McKay, a football game which dramatized, for me, three truths:

What a pretty game football is.

How pretty Los Angeles can be of a summer evening.

What a pretty fellow John McKay is.

We are going to miss him. His special talent was for answering dumb questions with a sort of reverse English that seemed to give the questions an *ex post facto* cleverness. No city can easily afford to lose a wit like that.

To enlighten those whose religion may be something other than football, John McKay is the former coach of the USC Trojans, who give us so much joy now and then by sacking Notre Dame and Ohio State. But we let him get away for a pittance—a mere dukedom in Florida—and now he is coach of the Tampa Bay Buccaneers.

Kickoff was at seven o'clock. It was the first game of the season, an event comparable, in the minds of some, with Easter. As the time drew near, the sun hung low in the sky over the west rim of the Coliseum, brassy and hot. The teams came out one by one to exercise on the turf, like ballet dancers taking their stretches, and then they trotted off, with the lithe, elastic grace of super athletes, and the marching bands and majorettes came out for a final pregame hymn.

A soprano took the field to sing "The Star-Spangled Banner," shooting the high notes like arrows into the reddening sky. She not only made it all the way up to the land of the free, there at the end, but actually shot past that target by at least four notes, a feat that could have been accomplished only with divine assistance.

In any game the kickoff is a ceremonial moment. Like a high priest spellbinding the multitudes, the placekicker sets the ball in its little cup and walks back a few paces, while every eye is on him, then trots toward the ball with exquisite timing and sends it arching through the sky, end over end, to set the game in motion.

Tampa Bay kicked off, Los Angeles fumbled, and the season had begun.

With binoculars I found John McKay on the far side of the field among his players. White hair, white shirt, white shoes, light gray pants, orange belt. A tidy man, pacing with neat short steps, bare arms folded. He looked quite pretty, like some exotic white-crested Florida cockatoo. He had been asked what he'd say if he lost this game, his first in the pros. What he'd say, he said, was, "I'll be darned."

It was only an exhibition game, of course, and exhibition games lack the awful tension and sense of grave consequence that invest a regular season game. It is something, I imagine, like watching an ancient religious sacrifice in which the victim is not really a live virgin.

But it was a beautiful dress rehearsal. The sun vanished at last. The low clouds turned from pink to salmon to magenta. The sky was the color of dark tea. The mountains were still visible across the city to the north. Above the peristyle a pale fire burned in the Olympic torch. The Rams, in blue and gold, and the Buccaneers, in orange and white, made ever-shifting patterns against the light-green turf, enigmatic but profoundly logical. Chuck Knox and John McKay, like God, had their reasons.

At halftime the lights were turned out for the lighted-match ceremony, in which everyone in the stadium is asked to light a match or a cigarette lighter on the count of three. It is a demonstration of the power people have when acting in concert. But this year (or did I only imagine it?) the flames seemed more scattered than dense. Had that many people quit smoking?

The fireworks display was splendid. One after another the bright flowers bloomed in the sky above the peristyle, gaudy and frenzied, with a crazy geometry in their patterns, like well-executed double reverses. Rockets exploded with the sound and concussion of five-inch guns; beautiful as it was, I was glad when it was over. The sound of heavy gunfire always makes me feel hollow and vaguely doomed.

In the second half the game flattened out. That was because you knew the Rams had it won, and being only an exhibition game it didn't really matter anyway, not in heaven.

There was a moment of rapture, though, when the Buccaneers executed a play that seemed to blossom like the halftime fireworks, the ball finally being thrown fifty yards across the field, kitty-cornered, for a long gain, almost to the goal line. It was John McKay's signature, like one of those vignettes in which Alfred Hitchcock signs his pictures. But then the Bucs fumbled and the Rams went on to win it, 26-3.

I was glad to read in the paper the next morning that Tampa Bay had played a stronger game than the score suggested and that when it was over, John McKay had said, "I looked pretty tonight, didn't I?"

All I can say is, I'll be darned.

14
The Chicken Little Syndrome

POPP'S REPORT

"Law enforcement straight out of
George Orwell's 1984 . . ."

Once again a newspaper columnist from east of the Mississippi has come to visit here in Southern California and then hurried home, like Chicken Little, with the gratifying news of our imminent self-destruction.

This time the messenger of doom is Bob Popp of the East Liverpool (O.) *Evening Review*, which offers "complete news coverage" of East Liverpool, Wellsville, Midland, Chester and Newell. These towns are not in England, as I might have guessed, but in the Ohio Valley where Ohio, Pennsylvania and West Virginia come together.

Whatever the problems of East Liverpool and its neighbors, they are not likely to suffer an exodus of residents to Southern California after reading Bob Popp's report. Flood, cyclone, ice and snow would seem like amiable alternatives to the appalling vision of Greater Los Angeles depicted in his column, "Snap, Crackle by Popp."

Popp himself sent me the column, along with a friendly note that shows he isn't angry, just sorry.

"Nowhere," he says in the column, "has the change been so rapid and so disheartening as it has been in this land of promise, this land of eternal sunshine, bright clear skies and fresh air. . . . On most days smog hangs like a dark impenetrable curtain on the horizon, so that it is impossible to see the tops of the snow-capped mountains. . . .

"Traffic has been slowed to a crawl on the celebrated freeways during the rush hours. Where once Californians drove like demons, at speeds of up to 80 miles an hour, the autos are jammed so thickly now that a veteran counts himself lucky if he is able to maintain a steady 30-mile-an-hour pace.

"Areas in which the housing was brand, spanking new 20 years ago have degenerated into modern-day slums, complete with boarded-up windows in repossessed homes, overgrown lawns and shrubbery; abandoned hulks of autos and—the worst scar of all—obscene words painted in the fiery colors of spray cans on the walls of buildings.

"Such rapid degeneration would be unthinkable in the East, which takes 100 years to develop a slum that the Los Angeles area could produce in a fifth of the time. . . .

"Perhaps the most chilling touch of all," he goes on, "is a law enforcement straight out of George Orwell's *1984.* A police helicopter circles endlessly at low altitude over residential areas at night, on the hunt for prowlers and also to assist in a search for lawbreakers if they are flushed from cover. It beams to the ground a high-intensity searchlight that roves constantly over the landscape, illuminating everything it touches with a brightness that seems like midday. . . .

"All this in a land that was noted not long ago for the fact that its residents left home without locking their doors and the only light that beamed down from the skies was the unobscured brilliance of stars and the moon. . . ."

I try not to react defensively to such observations as Popp's. Like the landscapes of Dali and the visions of Kafka, they may be distorted, but they seek out and illuminate our darker truths, as our helicopters seek out and illuminate our cowering felons.

We must not pretend we don't have any sores. San Francisco did that for years, and now the poor old girl is almost all sores. But we ought to treat our visitors better than Popp was treated. From what he describes, I would guess that he stayed with relatives who live on the wrong side of the old P.E. tracks and for entertainment they took him downtown and back on the Harbor Freeway at five o'clock of a Tuesday afternoon during an atmospheric inversion.

If he only knew it, he was lucky. He might have seen things that other visitors have found even more appalling than smog, traffic and decay. He might have gone to the Big A and watched Nolan Ryan lose his fifth straight game. Quite demoralizing. He might have gone to a swap meet in the Rose Bowl on a Sunday morning, when everybody back home in the Ohio Valley was in church, and seen American culture at its lowest level. He might have had to spend a night in the Beverly Hills Hotel, from where, as the Neil Simon character noted, "the whole place smells like an overripe cantaloupe."

At least Popp gave us credit for developing slums faster than our big cities do in the East, and of course that's good. A twenty-year-old slum is better to live in than a one-hundred-year-old slum and easier to dispose of without a lot of sentimental foot-dragging by historical societies.

Popp was a lot easier on us than most of our distinguished visitors. Just the other day the once angry young British playwright John Osborne went home to London, after a sojourn in the Beverly Hills Hotel, and said Los Angeles was so terrible he almost wished the Russians would atom-bomb it.

Once you've been here, though, you never quite get over it. I wouldn't be surprised if Osborne's next play smelled something like an overripe cantaloupe.

Journalists from other parts of the country who visit Los Angeles and then go home and write about what a dreadful place it is are always taking a risk of backfire from someone who lives in Los Angeles now but used to live where *they* came from and knows how black the pot is, as well as the kettle.

Having never been in the Ohio Valley, I wasn't able to give it back to him in kind when Bob Popp of the East Liverpool *Evening Review* took a quick look at Los Angeles and hurried back to tell the hometown folks of its appalling deterioration.

I try not to resent the fun our visitors have at our expense. Criticism doesn't hurt us, really, and might do us some good. Anyway, I always remember that *they* have to go back where they came from, while I get to stay here. They're entitled to some consolation.

But people who have lived in the places the visitors come from are not so tolerant. In Los Angeles you can find somebody from everywhere, and we are not without our immigrants from East Liverpool and its sister towns. I have heard from several of them, and they can hardly contain their indignation over Popp's remarks.

"Mr. Popp forgot to mention," observes my colleague Osgood Carruthers, "that the more sprawling industrial towns of the Ohio Valley—bigger than the charming, backward little hicksvilles his paper serves—were slums the day they were built."

"Honest to God, Jack," says Bob Lobdell, another fellow worker at the *Times*, "one would have to have seen East Liverpool to appreciate the full obtusity of columnist Popp's comments about Los Angeles. East Liverpool is an ugly city—one of the world's ugliest. I lived near it in Youngstown for eight years. Dank, dirty, dreary, dilapidated . . . East Liverpool is damn near the end of the world. It rates right up there with Steubenville, another Ohio River town. Knowing East Liverpool, I can't believe this turkey."

"We have been through Pennsylvania, West Virginia and Ohio," writes V. K. Schnitzel, "and the areas we saw weren't so great either. Smelly, dirty mining towns, bad roads, and drivers that would scare a diamond lane veteran. The Eastern slums make ours look like middle-class housing or better.

"Someone should invite Mr. Popp out in the winter when it's clear, and take him up on Angeles Crest and through Beverly Hills and along the coast and around Palos Verdes Peninsula and even out into the desert. Then send him home and tell him to look around. . . ."

"Bob Popp must either wear rose-colored glasses or suffer severe myopia when he makes his appointed rounds of the tri-state area," says a reader in Oxnard. "His beat is filled with eyesores. Without leaving the main streets you are confronted (or affronted) by tumbledown abandoned buildings (or have they fallen into the category of picturesque?), great mountains of waste from brick works, steel works, and pottery works. . . .

"As for Big Brother in the sky [our police helicopters, which reminded Popp of *1984*], I'd rather know he's looking than try to successfully negotiate passage through some of the speed traps they have set up for out-of-state cars in his area."

"I am a transplanted resident of the Ohio Valley," said Lois Barrus of Acton. "I was born and grew up in the area he came from. Mr. Popp has a lot of nerve talking about not being able to see the sun in Los Angeles. . . . The only sun you ever see in that area is through a cloud of smoke. . . . True, towns don't degenerate in that valley, they are simply obliterated and boarded up as the steel mills need more room to make longer girders. . . . And what is more terrifying than the state police officers with revolvers so long they hang below their shiny black boots! I'll take a helicopter any day."

"I was raised in Chester and my husband was raised in Newell," writes Gayle Wheatley. "My parents still live in Chester and on my visit last year I couldn't believe what those people have to put up with. Because one of our bridges was condemned, all the tri-state area has to use one bridge which is connected on both sides by a one-lane road that runs along the river. Men work on the road 24 hours a day and have for years, to keep the road from falling in the river. [It] goes on every night, all night. . . . I travel the freeway here every day and have never seen a mess like that. . . .

"Then there's the smog. It's a new problem but it's bad. . . . You can write your name on the furniture and your finger will be black. . . .''

A EULOGY TO L.A.

*"Her gift is especially apparent when applied
to our freeways."*

Los Angeles has been "done" again, this time by the English writer Jan Morris, and if Morris is right, we can put aside another of the clichés that we seem to inspire. Los Angeles is no longer the City of the Future, nor even of Now. We have already passed our prime. We were the city of the '40s and '50s, when America believed in machines and Know-How. Los Angeles today is a monument to that faith.

Morris has written our eulogy in the July issue of *Rolling Stone* under the title "L.A. Turnoff: Driving Through the Days of Future Passed." (Republished in *Destinations*, by Jan Morris, Oxford University Press.)

"Whatever happens to L.A.," she tells us, "it will always be the city of the automobile and the radio, show biz and the Brown Derby restaurant, the city where the American ideal of happiness by technique found its folk art in the ebullience of

Hollywood. It is essentially of the '40s and '50s, and especially perhaps of the World War II years, when the American conviction acquired the force of a crusade, and sent its jeeps, its technicians and its Betty Grables almost as sacred pledges across the world. Los Angeles then was everyone's vision of the New World: and so it must always remain, however it develops, a memorial to those particular times, as Florence means for everyone the spirit of Renaissance, and Vienna speaks always of *fin de siècle.*"

Morris is a brilliant writer and observer. I doubt if Los Angeles has ever been caught in such kaleidoscopic phrases, such opulent paragraphs, such illuminated metaphors. She probes metaphysical depths I hardly knew were there, and pops up, as flushed and breathless as a skin diver, with amazing fish. There is no sanctuary of the Los Angeles mystique to which she is not privy. She is able to psychoanalyze Ed Davis after one visit in his office and to reflect, at breakfast in Schwab's drugstore, that Lana Turner was discovered right there while "sitting on a bar stool."

Her gift is especially apparent when applied to our freeways: "These remain the city's grandest and most exciting artifacts. . . . They are inescapable, not just visually, but emotionally. . . . To most strangers they suggest chaos, or at least purgatory. . . . There comes a moment, though, when something clicks in one's own mechanism, and suddenly one grasps the rhythm of the freeway system, masters its tribal or ritual forms, and discovers it to be not a disruptive element at all, but a kind of computer key to the use of Los Angeles. . . . The moment this first happened to me, Los Angeles happened, too, and I glimpsed the real meaning of the city, and realized how firmly it had been disciplined by the rules of its own conviction."

I am not sure what that last sentence means, but I am often obliged to stay behind when Morris soars or plunges. Alas, I have never yet glimpsed the real meaning of the city.

Though given to shimmering insights, she also sees what ought to be plain to every other journalist but is almost always overlooked: "Expertise is the stock in trade of this metropolis, and behind the flash and the braggadocio, solid skill and scholarship prosper. There are craftsmen everywhere in L.A., craftsmen in electronics, in film-making, in literature, in social science, in advertising, in fashion. They say that in San Francisco there is less than meets the eye; in Los Angeles there is far more. . . ."

But she finds Los Angeles "charmless really, humorless, often reactionary, a city without a gentry." Still, we are not quite dead. "Nobody driving down Wilshire Boulevard, say, or watching the surfers spring into the Pacific, could call the culture of L.A. dead. It is full of vitality still, full of fun and wealth. . . . The refugees are still flocking to this haven beyond the deserts, the men of brilliance are still at work in laboratories and studios from Malibu to Irvine. Almost every development of Western thought . . . finds its niche, its expression and its encouragement somewhere in this metropolis. . . ."

But . . . "It is past its prime already. It has lost the exuberant certainty that made it seem even when I first knew it, unarguably the City of the Future, the City that Knew How. . . ."

We should be grateful to Morris for writing of Los Angeles as if it mattered, living or dead. But I feel like Tom Sawyer at his own funeral. I have this notion that the eulogy is premature.

If Los Angeles is still a haven for the brilliant and hopeful, a matrix for every development of Western thought, how can we be sure it is past its prime, a self-made monument to the war, mechanical know-how and Betty Grable?

Morris may be right about all these things, of course. I am not seer enough to say. But I do know she's wrong on one point, at least. Lana Turner was *not* sitting on a bar stool in Schwab's drugstore when she was discovered, as every schoolgirl now knows.

15

Newspaper Days

THE BLACK DAHLIA

"It was that name that set this one off."

Cecil Smith, our television critic, noted in the *Times* the other day that a TV movie is being made about the Black Dahlia murder case, and I was reminded of what was perhaps my finest hour as a newspaperman.

For those who missed Smith's story and weren't here to read the millions of words of lurid prose poured out by the local press at the time, the Black Dahlia was the nickname of a movie-struck small-town Maine girl who came to Hollywood in the late 1940s, drifted for a time in the backwash and ended up on a vacant lot one morning—nude, mutilated and cut in two.

There were four downtown newspapers (the late *Mirror* had not yet appeared) on that January morning in 1947 when Elizabeth Short's body was discovered, and for months to come they engaged in a raucous, sleepless and exhausting crusade to keep the public informed around the clock of every clue, every false trail, every suspect, every pertinent and impertinent piece of evidence and every conjecture even remotely connected with the Black Dahlia and her unpleasant end. It was *The Front Page* come to life.

I happened to be working on the rewrite desk of the *Daily News* that morning and drew the story when our police beat phoned in the first bulletin. Within the minute I had written what may have been the first sentence ever written on the Black Dahlia case. I can't remember it word for word, but my lead went pretty much like this: "The nude body of a young woman, neatly cut in two at the waist, was found early today on a vacant lot near Crenshaw and Exposition Boulevards."

I tore the copy out of my typewriter and took it up to the city editor, who was eager to get the story moving into type. He raced through the two lines, pencil poised, and wrote in a single word. I was annoyed. I thought that lead was damn near perfect.

Later, when the next edition came up from the pressroom, I grabbed a copy to see what he had done. It now read like this: "The nude body of a beautiful young woman, neatly cut in two at the waist, was found early today on a vacant lot near Crenshaw and Exposition Boulevards."

So the victim was beautiful. Our city editor, of course, no more knew what the unfortunate young woman had looked like than I did. But the lesson was clear. On the *Daily News*, at least, all young women whose nude bodies were found in two pieces on vacant lots were beautiful. I never forgot it.

In the days and weeks and months to come, as the police backtracked on Elizabeth Short's unhappy trail through the seedier layers of the Hollywood scene, hardly a reporter in town was denied the privilege of serving the public's right to know who Elizabeth Short had been and who had treated her so poorly. I'm sure that more reporters were assigned to the case than policemen, and in fact the policemen often got in our way.

One of the problems for newspapers was reporter retrieval. Young men turned loose in the Hollywood underground with an expense account were sometimes more enthusiastic in their investigations than their editors might have wanted, especially those who happened to encounter one of the more pliable of Miss Short's former girlfriends.

Once when we failed to hear from a legman for a week we sent a supposedly more trustworthy man out to bring him in, but the second man also vanished into the milieu, and as far as I know has never been heard from since.

In his story Cecil Smith quoted Detective Harry Hansen as saying: "There were other crimes as heinous and other victims as pretty and none of them got anywhere near the attention this killing got. It was that name that set this one off: The Black Dahlia."

I have always supposed that I was the first one to get "the Black Dahlia" into print, though I didn't make it up. As I remember, one of our reporters picked up a tip that Miss Short had frequented a certain Long Beach drugstore for a time. I looked the number up in the phone book and got the drugstore and talked to the pharmacist.

Yes, he remembered Elizabeth Short. "She used to hang around with the kids at the soda fountain. They called her the Black Dahlia—on account of the way she wore her hair."

The Black Dahlia! It was a rewrite man's dream. The fates were sparing of such gifts. I couldn't wait to get it into type.

Alas, in his story Cecil Smith gives credit for the Black Dahlia label to Bevo Means, who was then a police reporter for the *Herald-Express*. Bevo is an old and cherished friend of mine, a reporter of the old school. He could have played Hildy Johnson without reading the script. If Means wants credit for the Black Dahlia, I don't intend to challenge him. He's welcome.

But it's kind of like losing the Pulitzer Prize.

THE FRONT PAGE

"The women were just as able, tacky and dissolute
as the rest of us."

Television's new prime-time cultural hero this fall, according to the previews, will be the newspaper reporter. "First it was the thundering hooves of a posse of Wyatt Earps and Paladins," one magazine says, "then the whine of police sirens in a dozen cops-and-robbers series. This season it'll be the tap-tap-tap of the city room typewriter. . . ."

I can't help feeling a certain gratification at this news. At last the newspaper reporter, so long disdained by the true professionals with whom his work often brought him into contact—lawyers, detectives, criminals, politicians—is to be admitted to their status.

This new respect for us once-grubby tradesmen is plainly just another of the many fringe results of Watergate, and the new image of the reporter as projected by Woodward and Bernstein in their book, and by Redford and Hoffman in the movie *All the President's Men.*

Thanks are due mostly to the movie, I suppose, for no matter how hard the director tried for realism, Woodward and Bernstein were supposed to look like heroes, sort of, so they are portrayed as sober, literate and clean, if not tidy, and are not allowed to grind their cigarettes out in the carpet.

All of us are what we are in America because of the movies that shaped our characters and lighted our ambitions in our formative years; but few people can single out, as positively as I can, the one movie that was the pilot star of their lives. My movie was *The Front Page,* which came out in 1931, when I was a schoolboy, and gave me a call as powerful as the call of the cloth to an altar boy. I wanted to be a newspaperman like Hildy Johnson and nothing was going to stand in my way, not even marriage and World War II.

The Front Page turned up on TV the other night and it gave me an extraordinary chance to examine, from the perspective of what many would call a misspent life, the work of art that fired my clay. It was like that moment of revelation on the psychiatrist's couch, when suddenly a curtain is drawn back and the patient discovers the seed of all his trouble.

I was naturally dismayed to discover that the man who had been my inspiration was brash, childlike and maudlin and that the environment that was in my eyes Camelot—a criminal courthouse pressroom of the 1920s—was bleak, seedy and foul. I don't know why this should have come as any surprise, though, because I did go on to become brash, childlike and maudlin and functioned happily in pressrooms that were bleak, seedy and foul, right here in the Los Angeles of the late 1940s and the 1950s.

It is perhaps a tribute to the integrity of good human potential that so many other journalists who must have been exposed to Hildy Johnson turned out to be mature, distinguished and wise, like Eric Sevareid and Walter Cronkite. It is not necessarily true that "as the twig is bent, so shall the tree incline."

We have come a long way from the days of *The Front Page.* But all the credit can't go to Watergate, even though it did illuminate the role of the press in keeping the government fairly honest and reveal the reporter as hard-working and half-way intelligent, as well as creepy.

Actually, newspaper reporters have always been like that. It wasn't their character that gave them such a bad name; it was their life-style and their philosophy. They were so poorly paid they could never quite afford suburban middle-class entanglements, and their work made them associates if not allies of quacks, shysters, con men, hookers, embezzlers, ax murderers, politicians and other reporters, and their only friends were bartenders. Naturally they developed thin shells of cynicism to shield their mushy sentimental centers.

Back in the 1940s, I think it was, when every city room still had its Hildy Johnson, *The New Yorker* published a cartoon that showed half a dozen young men loitering on the steps of a college building in rumpled clothes with loosened neckties, hats on the back of their heads and cigarettes hanging from their lips. Over the doorway was engraved the legend SCHOOL OF JOURNALISM.

That cartoon was very significant. Its point was that now, in the era after World War II, would-be newspaper reporters were actually going to college, but they still tried to look as if they had been pulled out of the soup line in front of the rescue mission. As it so often did in those days, *The New Yorker* had neatly noted a cultural trend.

So the transformation which, it appears, will soon be documented on prime time began long before Watergate. It cannot be linked, either, to the increasing presence of women in the city room. A reporter is a reporter, whether man or woman. We had lots of women around when I was a young reporter and I can say for them that they were just as able, tacky and dissolute as the rest of us. (One thing different about today's women reporters is that some of them refer to themselves as "newspersons," as if the word "reporter" itself were either sexist or otherwise offensive. Thank God H. L. Mencken isn't alive to see "newspersons" in print.)

The change was accelerated in the 1950s with the general national affluence and the rise in a reporter's pay to rank with that of his friend the bartender. It was in this era that reporters began to go into respectable debt, acquiring automobiles and homes and even joining country clubs.

It was not long before his death in the 1950s, in fact, that

Mencken himself deplored this amalgamation of his own kind into the general culture. "Why, there are reporters today," he said in his one and only interview on radio, his voice gravid with revulsion, "who play *golf!*"

REPORTERS I HAVE KNOWN

*"There were a few who stood above their
unsavory fellows."*

In reading Cecil Smith's television column the other day I was pleased to find a letter from one of my old city editors, Chuck Chappell, assuring Smith that there really were newspapermen who wore their hats at their desks.

The question had arisen in a previous column Smith had written about the authenticity of character and atmosphere in the *Lou Grant* show, whose background is a fictional Los Angeles newspaper called the *Tribune.*

In his letter Chappell observed that when he was city editor of the *Daily News* here in the late 1940s at least three men wore their hats at the copy desk. "They were obviously holdovers from another era even then," he said, "and certainly would have no place in a current television series."

"I don't remember the hat wearers at the *Daily News,*" Smith replied, "but I do remember dropping by one time and seeing a couple of guys in the city room who were not wearing shirts. Hot day, as I recall."

Yes, it was a hot day. I was there. I had my shirt on, but I was sitting next to a man who didn't. Not only did he have his shirt off but also his undershirt. His name was Dwiggins, and he was the fastest man on a typewriter I ever saw in a city room. Dwig had just come in from a fire in the mountains and had peeled off his shirt to write his story in comfort. At one side of his typewriter were his notes (not a notebook but a sheaf of folded copy paper) and on the other a brown paper sack containing two or three cans of cold beer. Dwig had opened one of the cans, and as he worked he periodically removed it from the sack, took a swig and put it back in the sack. This was done to hide the beer from the city editor, not because he would have objected but because he might have commandeered a can.

Dwiggins was not at all eccentric. A saner, more stable man would be hard to imagine. As an example of his poise I remember the time he took me up in his little airplane, a two-seat war-surplus trainer. Suddenly, to my terror, as I felt the Gs increasing at the seat of my pants, I realized we were looping the loop—2,000 feet above Van Nuys.

"Damn you, Dwiggins," I screamed at him over the intercom when we had leveled out and I had got my breath back. "What if I hadn't had my seat belt fastened!"

His voice came back calmly: "Don't worry. Centrifugal force will hold you in."

Dwiggins liked to cover out-of-town stories, such as train wrecks, because he could fly himself to the scene. He would figure out where to land when he got there, and of course he was sometimes obliged to improvise. These flights were not authorized by the city desk, however, because Chuck Chappell was afraid that sooner or later Dwiggins would crash into somebody's barn, himself surviving, of course, and try to put the airplane on his expense account.

Actually, while reporters were generally a tacky-looking breed in my day, excepting such fashion plates as Tom Towers, photographers were inclined to be snappy dressers. Being dependent on precision equipment, they tended also to be precise about their appearance, favoring color-coordinated shirts, suits, neckties and cufflinks. Some of them even affected matching silk handkerchiefs and were careful about their socks.

There were a few reporters, though, who stood above their unsavory fellows, not only in dress but also in demeanor. I remember one first-class rewrite man on the old *Examiner* who put on such a moral front that he dared to be haughty and superior in the presence of his city editor, a reformed drunk whose tyranny was legendary.

On one occasion the city editor was standing at his desk and reading aloud from one of those quizzes which denote, if one answers enough questions *yes*, that one is an alcoholic.

" 'Do you ever drink in the morning?' " the tyrant barked,

so that every ear in the city room could hear. "Yes. . . . 'Do you often drink alone?' Yes! . . . 'When drinking, do you tend to seek companions of a lower social level?' Yes! . . ."

At this point, in the tremulous silence that followed the question, the rewrite man looked up from his typewriter, shot his immaculate cuffs and said: "Where ever do you find them?"

Then he arose, put on his hat and sauntered out, obviously on his way to the nearby saloon.

This fastidious chap was a New Yorker, by the way, and could be a bit tedious, when in his cups, on the subject of New York's superiority. Inevitably, someone asked him why, if he liked it so much better there, he didn't go back.

"Why, because," he said, arching an eyebrow to indicate his surprise that anyone should have to ask, "the Rocky Mountains are too steep on this side."

They get steeper every year.

16

The Sound of Music

THE MESSIAH AT OXY

"I was just passing by," he said, "and . . . wow!"

The music students at Occidental College were singing the second half of Handel's *Messiah* the other day at noon in the chapel and I went up to listen.

It was the morning after the rain, and I parked on a street that was strewn with wet sycamore leaves and walked up Alumni Avenue to the campus. The eucalyptus trees shone in the clean sky and scented the air. The fountain on the terrace was in full bloom.

I had a few minutes, so I walked over the quad and sat on a bench across from the student union. A girl sat on the wall behind the bench talking with a boy. There was an economics book on the wall beside her, and the boy periodically slapped his thigh with a thick copy of *The United States and China.* They didn't seem to be discussing either subject.

I ventured into the student union to look at the ads tacked up on the bulletin board. FOR SALE—'71 Porsche, green and brown, with special wheels . . . a ¼-keg beer tapper . . . summer sessions in Guadalajara . . . a chance to help children learn to read . . . a European exploration tour . . . TYPING—fast, accurate; spelling and simple grammar slips corrected . . .

I was headed for the chapel when I heard a cry of "Dr. Johnson" behind me. I turned. She faced me breathlessly.

"Dr. Johnson," she said, "are you going to teach Organic Two again?"

"No," I said, "I'm afraid I'm not Dr. Johnson."

"Oh," she said. She sounded disappointed. So was I, rather.

I strolled on, buoyed up by the discovery that, from the rear at least, I could be mistaken for a college professor.

The singers were hurrying to the chapel from their classes. I stopped a moment at the door, catching bits of conversation.

"You know," a boy was saying, "it's like, when you die . . ."

"Uh huh," said the girl at his side, evidently knowing.

Behind them, a girl walking alone held a large red sycamore leaf by the stem, like a bouquet.

Inside the chapel, a young man with a Vandyke beard was passing out tattered songbooks.

"Are you going to sing with us?" he asked me, perhaps mistaking me for Dr. Johnson.

"No," I said, "I came to listen."

"We'd like to have you sing with us. Everybody sings. But you're welcome in any capacity."

The chapel is a jewel, shaped like a cross and lighted softly by sunlight through stained glass. It was all very casual, a chorus of students in corduroys or short skirts or worn blue jeans.

"Let's pick up where we left off," said the bearded young man. He introduced the pianist and then the first soloist, a bass. *For behold*, he sang, *darkness shall cover the earth . . .*

There was applause when he finished, and I remembered how often I had restrained myself from applauding a well-sung hymn in church, or shouting "Bravo!"

A girl with a sweet soprano voice and pale gold hair down to her shoulders sang a solo of rejoicing, holding her book high, elbows out, swaying slightly with the rhythm of the hymn, and for a moment it was hard not to believe in angels.

Everyone stood—"quickly," as the book instructed—for *Glory to God in the highest, peace on earth, goodwill towards men. . . .*

Finally the director said, "Guess what we're going to do now?"

They stood and sang that magnificent chorus, the young voices eager and buoyant, and at the height of it, with the hallelujahs ringing out, a boy slipped in and sat on the bench beside me. He seemed in awe.

When the last "hallelujah" died he turned to me. *"How beautiful!"* he whispered. "What *is* it?"

"The *Messiah*," I said. "Handel's *Messiah*. The 'Hallelujah Chorus.' "

"I was just passing by," he said, "and . . . *wow!*"

"Hallelujah," I agreed and walked back to my car, breathing the scent of eucalyptus and kicking sycamore leaves and wondering what Organic 2 was all about.

HOLLYWOOD BOWL

"Why does the satyr always get the blame?"

We shared a box at the Hollywood Bowl with friends last Thursday and it turned out to be one of those evenings where everything seems right, from the wine to the last bravo; and I capped it with an excellent spoonerism, my first in years.

Like every good spoonerism it was unconscious, a slip of the tongue, so I am really not entitled to any credit; but it was so apt and beguiling that I will always remember it with an author's pride.

Ruth Vincent was our hostess and her other guests were Robert Nathan and his wife Anna Lee. Mrs. Vincent had driven up from her house in Baja with fresh scallops cooked in lemon juice, my wife brought a green salad and a clutch of extremely dainty cucumber sandwiches, and the Nathans brought the wine, a white Burgundy, Pouilly-Fuissé 1969.

I have experienced nights at the Bowl that were more beautiful and moving, like the night Itzhak Perlman played a Mozart concerto under a full moon that had only recently been walked on by two Americans. That night had given me a sense of oneness with the universe; this night made me feel thirty years old again. Feeling thirty is better than feeling as one with the universe.

The first piece on the program was a Mozart overture: brief, light, sportive. It set the tone for the evening. The conductor was a Frenchman, Jean-Pierre Rampal, the celebrated flutist. He looked slightly dissolute and mischievous, despite his white jacket and black tie, like some not altogether trustworthy prestidigitator one might meet in a novel by Simenon. One knew we would get no solemnity from *his* baton.

After the Mozart, M. Rampal came out with a flute, and it
turned out he was the soloist for the evening as well as the
conductor. He played a Vivaldi concerto with breathtaking virtuosity, simultaneously directing the orchestra with body English.

After being driven offstage by applause he returned with
Zita Carno to attempt the duo for flute and piano by Copland.
The music was as wild as two bats in a cave: primitive, complex, unpredictable, exciting. There was a breeze in the Bowl,
and to keep his music from blowing away M. Rampal had
fastened it to the stand with clothespins, or what looked to me
like clothespins, and occasionally the duet was suspended,
Miss Carno hovering over the keyboard like a hummingbird,
while the flutist reset his clothespins.

"You know," said Robert Nathan when it was over, "Copland has mad nightingales in his head."

But the apogee of the evening, and I say that even though
it was followed by Beethoven's Eighth symphony, was the
Concerto in G for two flutes and orchestra by Cimarosa, the
Italian Mozart, in which M. Rampal was joined by flutist Anne
Diener Giles.

"She handles her clothespins better than he does," my
wife whispered as the two of them fastened their music to the
racks.

It was a lovely piece, both innocent and erotic. M. Rampal
was the satyr, Miss Giles his prey. They had met in the woods
and fallen into a flirtation, talking with their flutes; but soon
they were talking with their bodies, too, like two white butterflies courting. The bent knees, the outthrust hip, the provoca-
tive shoulder turned away. Was Miss Giles the seduced, I began
to wonder, or the seducer? Why does the satyr always get the
blame?

"She has a sweeter flute than he has," Nathan said, when
the piece was over.

There were three curtain calls, cries of bravo and exuberant whistling, and a basket of flowers was thrust into Miss
Giles's hands.

Mrs. Vincent had brought along one of Nathan's books of
poetry as a gift for me, and at the intermission she asked him

to inscribe it. He consented, penning a new poem for the occasion above his signature.

> *I chose the high and lonely path*
> *Far up above the common lot.*
> *And so the lowliest poet hath*
> *What I have not.*

"I call it 'Fame,' " he said. "I wrote it just this morning. I had this picture of myself walking on a high wire, and suddenly there was no wire there."

Robert Nathan has nightingales in his head, but they aren't mad; they're merely enchanted.

After the concert we were trudging up the asphalt toward the car when I caught sight of Miss Giles a few steps ahead of me. She was laughing and tossing her long blond hair, and a girl was a step behind her with her basket of flowers. I hurried up to catch her; I had to let her know how I felt about her. But she is a leggy young woman, and I was burdened with a picnic basket on each arm. She got away.

I turned around to go back to my group. Nathan was right behind me. The others were out of sight in the crowd.

"What happened to *you?*" my wife asked when we found them.

"I was trying to catch Miss Giles," I said.

We'd said good night to the others and were on our way home when I recalled what Nathan had said about Miss Giles.

"She has a fluter sweet than he has," I said.

My wife didn't laugh. She understood me perfectly.

THE BILTMORE

"The Misses Phelps had arrived for the musicale, no doubt, in a Jordan roadster."

I hadn't been upstairs at the Biltmore since the Democratic convention of 1960, so I was happy to accept an invitation from friends to have brunch in their suite one Sunday and later to attend the tea and musicale downstairs.

Considering the Sunday afternoons I had spent in front of

my television watching football, the thought of a tea and musicale on a Sunday afternoon seemed quaint and appealing.

The suite was on Grand Avenue at the hotel's southwest
corner, and from the bay windows we looked down on the east
lawn of the library and up Grand to the Music Center, a view
that reassured me we were indeed in Los Angeles.

I will never again be in the Biltmore, I suppose, without
thinking of that morning when I watched from an upstairs
window on Olive Street as John Fitzgerald Kennedy arrived in
an open car to begin his conquest of the 1960 convention. The
crowd surged out into the street, engulfing the car, and the
candidate, hatless and grinning, stepped down into it and was
swallowed whole. It had seemed to me an ominous thing.

The musicale began at three o'clock. The Music Room, I
saw, was unchanged, except perhaps for a dusting, since the
morning Stuart Symington had taken it over for a festive reception, his final hopeless splurge before the Kennedys cut him
out like a bad calf.

Small tables had been set out around the grand piano, and
there were perhaps forty people seated when the Misses Stacy
and Sheila Phelps appeared in pale peach-colored flowered chif-
fon dresses, reminding me of pressed roses, and began their
recital, Miss Sheila Phelps at the piano, her sister playing the
violin. They seemed to be intense and serious young ladies, all
concentration, but I thought of Emily Dickinson, fire under
ice.

Surely, I imagined as they began to play, it could not be
1977, nor even 1957. The Beatles hadn't been born yet; neither
had Lee Harvey Oswald, Evel Knievel, Mick Jagger, William
Calley. The 1960s hadn't happened. Here was the elegant
Music Room, exactly as it was in 1925, with its crystal chandeliers, fluted columns, ornate ceiling and opalescent skylight.
Mr. Coolidge, that taciturn Yankee, was in the White House,
and the Misses Phelps had arrived for the musicale, no doubt,
in a Jordan roadster.

Quaint as it might have seemed, it was not long before the
young ladies had warmed up on Bach and Vivaldi and a Brahms
scherzo and thrown themselves into an ecstatic suite by Bloch,
playing with a passion and ferocity that seemed exquisitely
but just barely under control, like one of Miss Dickinson's
poems.

The audience sat as still as people in a movie freeze. They looked enchanted, as if they had never before heard sound that was not electronic and were afraid that a word, a cough, a scraping chair would scare it off.

After an interlude we were given a caprice by Paganini and some lollipops by Kreisler and a meditation by Glazunov, which evoked in me the strange habitual melancholy of a Sunday afternoon. Finally we were lifted again by a lively polonaise and then were loosed upon the tea and cakes.

Some Sunday afternoon in some November, when I am strapped to my chair by my own passions, helpless and anguished as once again I watch the Rams lie down and die in the snow before the Minnesota Vikings, perhaps I will think of the Music Room at the Biltmore and of the Misses Phelps playing Bach and Brahms and Paganini with such grace and spirit, far from the roar of the crowd, and wish I were there.

CHRISTMAS IN PERSHING SQUARE

*"He sang with his eyes shut, his face
swollen and purple."*

No matter how much I try to resist it, at least until Christmas Eve, the Yuletide spirit usually gets to me when I'm not expecting it, at some unguarded moment, from some improbable quarter.

I was ambushed by it the other day in downtown Los Angeles. I was not unaware of the seasonal seductions of that neighborhood. The elevators were playing carols. The store windows were festive. The Santa Belles were out on their corners, dancing to keep their legs warm and ringing their little bells. But I had steeled myself against these familiar sirens and thought I was safe when I took the shortcut through Pershing Square.

There was not much chance of catching the Christmas spirit from the shabby fringe of derelicts around the ornamental pool. They dozed in the sun, nipped from bottles in brown paper sacks, scanned remnants of discarded newspapers, quarreled with the pigeons and peered back into the hazy past, looking for some long-lost fork in the road.

Two men stood side by side in front of the war memorial singing "Silent Night." One was about five feet tall and wore a shapeless coat that would have looked big on Boris Karloff. The other wore a limp fedora that hid his face except for the mouth and a threadbare overcoat so large he didn't seem to be wearing it so much as living in it.

Their appearance alone might have attracted no attention in the park, being a kind of protective coloration; but their singing was hard to ignore, and now and then one of their captive audience would turn his head in their direction and stare in silent wonder.

The smaller man was the leader. He sang in a tenor voice that evidently had known much abuse and given vent to much anguish and passion. He worked it to the very edge of its capacity, rubbing its raw edge painfully against the underside of the high notes, falling heroically short of the Savior in "Christ the Savior is born" and sinking mercifully into "heavenly peace." He sang with his eyes shut, his face swollen and purple from the effort.

His partner wrestled the harmony with a mixture of foolhardiness and caution, like an over-the-hill matador fighting a mean young bull. His voice might have been deep and resonant once. It would come on strong for a phrase and then fade out. As he sang he rocked perilously back and forth, his open mouth vanishing under the brim of his hat when he bent forward and appearing in full flower for a moment on the backswing before rolling out of sight.

It wasn't simply the quality of their performance or the incongruity of their appearance that kept me there, but the growing realization that they didn't stop when they finished the song. They were no sooner through the final "heavenly peace" than the smaller man would throw his shoulders back, fill his lungs, turn himself purple, and start all over again:

> "Si . . . uh . . lent night!
> Ho . . . uh . . . ly night!"

His partner would turn to face him at each of these reprises as if stupefied by this new demand on his overextended powers. He would stand dumb until he made sure the song was launched again beyond recall, then once more he would lean backward, his gray mouth opening valiantly, and attack the harmony, not far off the pitch and almost on the beat.

> "All is calm,
> All is bright!"

They had sung it through three times and started again when I walked on to Fifth and Hill and beyond their reach, wondering at the indestructibility of the Christmas spirit. Evidently it was the only carol they knew, but it was a miracle, I thought, that even "Silent Night" had survived, fairly intact, the disenchantments they must have suffered.

I won't say that I myself was infused with the Christmas spirit by that threadbare "Silent Night," but I couldn't very well say "humbug" either. Nobody was going to take those old men riding through the snow on a one-horse open sleigh or stuff them full of plum pudding and fill their stockings with the things they wanted; yet they seemed to be bursting with good will anyway and were moved to spread it among their fellows.

What resistance I still had was caved in the next night when we drove up to Descanso Gardens for the preview opening of the annual Nine Days of Christmas at Hospitality House.

It was cold but exhilarating—something like riding in an open sleigh, I thought—as the tram took us from the gate to the house through tunnels of overhanging oaks. White camellias swam toward us through the dark, and here and there our headlights shone on clusters of red berries tacked to the trees.

We emerged from the oaks to see the lighted house, like a house in a fairy tale, and suddenly the night was filled with angelic singing. It came from a chorus of schoolchildren who stood outdoors, huddled together in their coats and mittens. An utterly disarming sound—sweet, vibrant, innocent and supple. No orchestra could simulate its poignancy, and only the most vigilant ear could catch its undercurrent of throttled mischief.

The house was warm and bright and crammed with handmade gifts and decorations and the sounds and scents of

Christmases past. A child who wakened to Christmas Day in a house like this, I thought, would never forget it, and fifty years later, long after he had taken some wrong fork in the road, he might stand in Pershing Square, wrapped in rags, and pour out the memory of it to the pigeons and the sky:

Silent night
Holy night.
I was hooked.

17

Hollywood Hot Spots...Past

BELLE OF THE HOLLYWOOD HOTEL

*"Male guests had to line up and take turns dancing her
around the lobby. . . ."*

A new generation inhabits Hollywood Boulevard these
days, and most of them probably have never heard of the Hollywood Hotel that once ornamented the boulevard between
Highland and Orchid avenues and whose destruction inspired
such sadness and nostalgia just twenty years ago.

As I remember it, the hotel was mission-Victorian in style,
if such a combination is possible, with a grab bag of arches,
balconies, turrets and cupolas and a broad veranda from which
its residents watched the life and death of a legend. The hotel
sat back from the street behind grass and was shaded by palm
trees whose uprooting caused more anguish than the razing of
the rambling old hotel itself.

What brings it to mind is a letter from a reader, Edward K.
Sprott, enclosing a copy of a letter evidently written by the
manager of the hotel to a Percy Williams of Tucson, Arizona,
on June 4, 1909.

"The original," Sprott writes, "was found in an oaken rolltop desk that for many years belonged to my grandfather. . . .
He bought the desk in 1920 from the gentleman to whom the
letter was addressed. I found the letter while reworking the
rolltop. . . . I thought you might get a kick out of the fact that
at one time one could 'see the ocean from the veranda.' How
many people today are familiar with the word veranda? And
how many people can see the ocean from any part of Hollywood?"

The letter was on the illustrated stationery of "The Hotel

of Hollywood," and it seems to prove that what I would have thought was a phenomenon of the electronic age—direct-mail advertising—was already a well-developed art in 1909.

"If we didn't think we had something unusually attractive in the way of hotel accommodations to offer," it began, "we wouldn't take the trouble to write this letter nor ask you to spend the time to read it, but just because we believe the Hollywood Hotel is out of the ordinary and will please you we are taking this means of calling your attention to it.

"Hollywood, as you no doubt are aware, is about halfway between Los Angeles and the ocean, nestling in the foothills of the Coast Range; the broad Pacific may be seen from the hotel veranda. You can reach Los Angeles, Ocean Park, Santa Monica or Venice in 20 minutes by new electric car service. Away from the dampness and fog, it is always swept by cool ozone-laden breezes, making it the most desirable summer resort on the Pacific Coast.

"We are pleased to give you our lowest summer rates as follows: American plan. Steam heat. Open all the year. Special rates to families. $13.50 per week for one person or $25 per week for two people in room with private bath.

"Hoping to have the pleasure of entertaining you here this summer, I am, yours very truly . . ."

I only vaguely remembered the hotel and the obsequies that had marked its demise, so to refresh my memory I called at the *Times* library and was assisted at the counter by a young woman I hadn't met before. I asked if I could see our file of clippings on the Hollywood Hotel.

She looked uncertain, evidently never having heard of the Hollywood Hotel.

"It was torn down years ago," I said. "But it was famous. There was a movie about it. *Hollywood Hotel.* You don't remember the song?"

She shook her head. I hummed a few bars. Ta ta ta . . . ta ta ta . . . ta ta ta . . . [and so on] . . . at the Holly*wood* Ho*tel!*"

She backed away. "I'll go look," she said.

I was right, of course. We did have a file under "Hollywood Hotel." There was a story by Cecil Smith about its memories and the famous people who had lived there or sat on its veranda or danced in its ballroom. Valentino. Nazimova. Dustin Farnum. Anita Stewart. Thomas Meighan. Flora Finch . . .

Carrie Jacobs Bond had composed "A Perfect Day" in the music room. Valentino had lived in Room 264 and honeymooned there with his first wife. Years later (it was said) she came to the hotel and asked to see the room . . . "and took one glance and left again. . . ."

The hotel's passing was eloquently noted, also, on our paper's editorial page: "There is something about the passing of old buildings that touches the heartstrings of community residents who have, as the saying goes, 'grown up' with them. The announcement that the Hollywood Hotel is to be razed to make way for a modern department store can, therefore, be expected to bring wistful memories to Hollywoodians who saw the present film capital emerge from the truck farms and barley fields.

"Although never actually the palatial and giddy establishment portrayed to the world in the memorable movie bearing its name, it has always had an atmosphere all its own. . . ."

Memorable movie? I don't know. Maybe it wasn't so memorable, if that young woman in our library had never heard of it.

Oh, well. She's probably never heard of Flora Finch, either.

I will always think of Ben Lyon as the dashing but doomed young flier in *Hell's Angels.* He had two great scenes in that classic, as I remember, one in which he was shot down by a German ace in an open Fokker and one in which he was shot down by Jean Harlow in an open peignoir.

I always liked Ben Lyon. He seemed so indestructibly fresh and debonair. So I was pleased the other day to hear from him and to be reminded that he had survived Miss Harlow and World War I and after a long sojourn in London was back in Hollywood again.

He was moved to write, he said, by my memoir on the old Hollywood Hotel, once the symbol of Hollywood style, which has been gone now for more than twenty years.

"It was every young actor's ambition to get to Hollywood," Ben recalls, "and mine came true July 4th, 1923. Having saved up enough money from Broadway plays to remain out here for a few months, I checked into the Hollywood Hotel, as the twenty-five-dollar-per-week American plan appealed not only to me but also to my pocketbook. What a thrill it was to be living under the same roof that had housed Valentino, Thomas Meighan, Charlie Farrell, Gilbert Roland and many other great stars!

"However, there was one catch which we all were aware of, and that was the Thursday-night dance in the lobby. The hotel was owned by an elderly, charming and buxom woman named Miss Hershey, who adored dancing to the three-piece orchestra. But she was not a Leslie Caron, Ginger Rogers, Ann Miller or Cyd Charisse. We young male guests had to line up and take turns dancing her around the lobby or chance being asked to give up our rooms. Needless to say we danced her.

"I don't recall seeing the ocean from the veranda. However, we could look across the street to a little shop on Highland Avenue where a small middle-aged man would personally mix several ingredients in a jar for your special makeup. . . . His name was Max Factor.

"Also across the street was Hellman's barbershop where you would always run into such stars as Richard Dix, Conrad Nagel or John Gilbert. It would not surprise you to see Tom Mix drive up in his big convertible with a saddle across the hood displaying the silver letters T.O.M. M.I.X. . . . And of course half a block south of the hotel was the famous Montmartre restaurant, where all the stars met every day for lunch and I met my present wife Marion Nixon. . . ."

I had never heard of the redoubtable Miss Hershey, belle of the Hollywood Hotel ballroom, so it seemed a neat coincidence when the name turned up again in a letter that came the same day from Dorothy Phillips, of Naples Island, Long Beach.

"Miss Hershey wintered in Long Beach many years ago," wrote Miss Phillips. "I guess Pennsylvania was too much for her in the winter. Well, she built a hotel here on Naples Island designed after the old Hollywood Hotel. Someone said that originally she owned the Hollywood Hotel. How true that is I don't know.

"Anyway, the hotel here on Naples was never occupied for 25 years except by her guests. Then during Prohibition days, when Naples was not in the city of Long Beach but in Los Angeles County, the hotel became a real gambling place like the ships three miles off the coast. At the present time there is an apartment building on the land where the hotel stood. Many old-timers here remember it well. The canal that led up to the hotel and brought gondolas full of people is filled in now. . . ."

There seems no doubt that the Miss Hershey of Naples and the Miss Hershey of Hollywood were the same, and from the recollections of Ben Lyon and Dorothy Phillips there emerges a gothic vision of the fun-loving spinster, no Leslie Caron, but tireless and inescapable, whirling her young hostages about the ballroom of the island stronghold she had built to keep them in.

The year before the Hollywood Hotel was torn down a young college man named Jimmy Hicks spent two weeks in it on summer vacation, just so he could say he had. "The Hollywood Hotel was of course more than a hotel," he writes. "It was a monument to a golden past and a reminder of the continuity of life. Its destruction marked the beginning of the decline of Hollywood. . . . We shall never see its like again. . . ."

"I recall driving past the fading façade of the Hollywood Hotel shortly after I came to Southern California," writes Gene Webster of KABC-TV, "and feeling somewhat awed, as if I were at the shrine of some ancient gods. . . ."

Webster says he knows how I felt when I found that one of our young librarians at the *Times* had never heard of the Hollywood Hotel. "I was clearing out an old filing cabinet and found in the back of a drawer an old copy of *TV-Radio Mirror*. On the cover was a picture of the star of the old CBS radio series *Halls of Ivy*. I picked it up and said, 'My gawd, Ronald Colman!' A dewy-faced young secretary at a desk nearby looked up with a blank expression and queried, 'Ronald who?' "

Oh, well. Don't worry, Gene. Don't worry, Ben. Don't worry, Ronald and Miss Hershey, wherever you are.

Someday a dewy young thing will look up and say, "Barbra who?"

Like many other early Hollywood figures whose legends are not preserved on film or in print, Miss Hershey might have faded entirely from memory, except for these few memoirs.

So I am delighted to have a letter about this formidable lady from Mary Loos, author of the Hollywood historical romance *The Beggars Are Coming*, who often visited her grandparents at the Hollywood Hotel when they lived there and she was a little girl. Being the niece of the piquant screenwriter and novelist Anita Loos, and very precocious, Mary Loos saw a great deal, evidently, and imagined what she had to.

"Mira Hershey was one of the few rich virgins of Hollywood," she says, making a presumption which I suppose only a very precocious little girl could have made. As a young woman Miss Hershey had studied music in Europe, she recalls, but her father went along as chaperon, and it was hotel gossip that when a young European invited her to an evening out her father said, "What time shall we pick you up?" And that was the last proposal Miss Hershey ever had.

But her European education had not been entirely fruitless. "She played the piano, and sometimes sat down and ripped off Bach with her nose held high. Now an old woman, with eyelids at half mast, a pince-nez low on her beaklike nose, she looked upon the passing scene with the detachment of a woman who had never been too personally involved with human relationships.

"She had a habit of stepping out on the veranda edging the curved palm-lined driveway to observe the leisurely flow of traffic. Her bifocals must have interfered with her perspective, for she was known to trip and fall down the steps. So their edges were painted white, and the little Filipino bellhops stood by to catch her if she fell. . . .

"Once a month she drove her electric automobile down to Spring Street to see her lawyers. She usually forgot where she parked it; and the police department was called to help her find it. It became a ritual, the police spotting it before the alarm was sent out by her law firm.

"Once she was sailing down Hollywood Boulevard with my grandmother and Mrs. Talmadge (the mother of the Talmadge girls). Miss Hershey grabbed the steering stick too hard, failed to negotiate a U-turn, and the car tipped over, slowly and majestically."

Besides the hotel, Miss Hershey owned the Hershey Arms, down by Westlake Park. Mary Loos's parents courted at the park, and her great-grandfather, O. T. Johnson, had a Victorian mansion with large gardens and iron stags on the lawn where Good Samaritan Hospital now stands.

Miss Hershey was evidently a trencherman who enjoyed the hotel's five-course American-plan meals, but she was reluctant to run up cleaning bills, and when a gravy spot appeared on her gown she would simply cover it with a brooch. "I remember thinking," recalls Mary Loos, "that she looked like a general with all her medals. . . .

"Every afternoon there was a free tea served in the spacious lobby. Damask napkins, gleaming silver and countless finger sandwiches, tarts and cookies were ritually served by the starched waitresses who also served meals in the dining room. They all seemed very old to me, and maybe they were, for they all had put their money in a bank presided over by a Mr. Beesemeyer. The bank went under with all their savings, so they went on working. . . .

"My grandmother sat on the spacious veranda overlooking Hollywood Boulevard in one of the two dozen sturdy rocking chairs, knitting and chatting with the likes of Mary Pickford's mother and the Talmadge girls' 'Peg' and other elders related to the successful people of the picture industry. . . .

"I can see my grandmother and Miss Hershey—all the old women—with a scattering of a few elderly dandies, rocking away in chairs stout enough to float them in a Johnstown flood. They all listened to each other's joys and braggadocio about the doings of their children and grandchildren, and they shared each other's woes and stepped into many a breach. It must have been a blessing to Miss Hershey, for it gave her a family. . . .

"So bless the memory of Mira Hershey. She probably hardly knew I existed, save to stop me from scooting across her polished floors to run out to the garden, where my favorite, Mr. Gallaudet, was allowed a little shop in a gardener's potting shed to pursue his hobby of stuffing birds.

"I think the ghosts of the Hollywood Hotel and Miss Hershey (no one ever dast call her Mira) still exist, when people who knew them halt momentarily at the stop signal at Hollywood and Highland. . . ."

If Miss Hershey was a pinchpenny in life, she was generous in her will. Thousands of UCLA students who have enjoyed the amenities of the coed dormitory Hershey Hall have perhaps been unaware that their benefactor was none other than Mira Hershey herself, belle of the Thursday-night ball in the Hollywood Hotel.

THE HOLLYWOOD CANTEEN

"He danced seven bars of 'Mairzy Doats'
with Shirley Temple."

Occasionally the same mail that brings me a question I can't answer also brings the answer, as if Random Chance, busy as He must be, had taken time out to give me a hand.

"Would you remember," asks a letter from H. Ward Kentnor of West Covina, "just where the Hollywood Canteen was at? Like yourself, I am an ex-GI. I was here in California early in '42, at Hueneme. One night we were brought to Hollywood by Greyhound (me and six buddies) and we found, on our own, the Hollywood Canteen. It was great.

"We danced, had coffee and sandwiches, and best of all, met the actors and actresses of that time. Ruth Roland, who talked to us for quite some time. Eddie Cantor, who started to wash some dishes, and many others. But where the ol' Canteen was at, I don't remember. . . . I am thinking maybe there are others who would like to know. . . ."

So it seemed almost more than coincidence a minute later when I opened a letter from Helen Tuthill Andrews of La Canada-Flintridge enclosing the 1943 edition of a pocket-size guide called *Sinning in Hollywood, for Servicemen Only.* The booklet had cost 25 cents and purported to give servicemen "the sinside dope" on the hot spots of Hollywood and Los Angeles, which was known in those wartime days as an *all reet* liberty town.

"I happened to find it in old bookstore years ago," the letter explained. "I doubt very much if there are many of them around today."

In a breezy style that still blows with the energy and exuberance of that turning-point year of the war, the booklet exhorted its readers: "All you jive-hungry, femme-starved disciples of the good Omar Khayyam who feel the need (and who does not?) for your loaf of bread, jug of wine, and thou, oh babe, gather around and harken to the beguiling and insinuating voice of temptation! We now begin with a tour of the Cheaper and Better Hot Spots. . . ."

In 1943 the cheaper and better hot spots included the It Cafe in the Hotel Plaza, Larry Potter's Stardust, on the boulevard at Wilcox, the Club Zarape, toward downtown on Sunset, and the Hofbrau Gardens, on Sunset near Vine (no cover, 25 cents minimum, dinner 85 cents).

For men with a taste for more exotic excitements the booklet recommended the Bamba Club and the Paris Inn downtown, the Tropics, at Sunset and Vine, and two oases which, thirty-three years later, are still there: Don the Beachcomber's (no cover, no minimum, dinner from $1.75) and the Seven Seas, across from Grauman's Chinese, where it used to rain on the half hour and maybe still does.

For the big spenders, the booklet listed the class joints, such as the Biltmore Bowl ($1 minimum, dinner from $2), the Mocambo, on the Strip ("a place to say you've been to, but bring along the bank roll—$1.50 cover, $2 on Saturday"), the Trocadero ("wallow in the stardust sprinkled about by the glamor-lovelies of the Hollywood firmament") and two more that are still there—the Zebra Room and the Coconut Grove ("come well-heeled and prepare to gape. Freddy Martin a fixture."). A fixture indeed; Freddy is still around and pops up at the Grove every now and then to play a special.

For laughs the booklet recommended the Radio Room, where an orchestra of maniacs was led by Mike Riley, the madman who wrote "The Music Goes Round," and Slapsie Maxie's, where you not only got to meet Slapsie Maxie himself but could also enjoy the comic genius of Ben Blue. (How I wish I could sit and watch Ben Blue for no cover, $1 minimum today!)

For Girls Girls Girls there was Earl Carroll's Theater Restaurant, through whose portals passed the most beautiful girls in the world; and the Florentine Gardens, where the girls were such "lissome lovelies" that a soldier might forget to eat his dinner.

Jitterbugging was still the most popular method of releasing energy in public, and it could be done at the Zenda on West

Seventh Street, at the Casino Gardens in Ocean Park (take red car from Subway Terminal at Fifth and Hill) and at the Aragon Ballroom on the pier, where you might even catch Cab Calloway or Louis Armstrong (admission 40 cents).

For men of a more studious nature, there were cultural attractions such as the Observatory and Planetarium, the La Brea tar pits, the alligator and ostrich farms and Forest Lawn (free).

But on to the question:

"At the intersection of Sunset and Cahuenga is the famous Hollywood Canteen," the booklet said, "where you feel like a king if you don't mind company. Every night in the week, but particularly on Saturday nights, you will be waited on by stars such as Charles Boyer, Hedy Lamarr, Betty Grable, Dorothy Lamour. You'll find scores of hostesses, including the stars, itching to jig with you, food cooked by other stars and excellent entertainment by still other stars and top name bands. Kay Kyser is almost always present—stoodents!"

There was one final word of caution: "Don't forget—the glare of klieg lights acts in the manner of a candle with moths, luring to the sidewalks of Hollywood the most beautiful and talented women in the world. . . ."

I suppose it all sounds rather innocent and vulgar from this distance. But don't forget, students, it won the war.

Old soldiers tend to romanticize all the bleak encounters of their lonely wartime liberties in strange cities, so I am not surprised to find that the Hollywood Canteen, where the GIs went to dance with the stars, was not as glittering as some of them remember it.

The other day I quoted from a vintage serviceman's guide which suggested that a decent boy from Iowa, on the way out to fight for his country, might drop in at the Canteen on a Saturday night and find himself in the arms of Rita Hayworth.

Alas, I have now heard from some other veterans—the hard-working stenos and not quite starlets who really staffed the Canteen and did the dishes, while the stars made spot appearances with their press agents and slipped away without breaking a fingernail.

"I was a secretary at Columbia Pictures then," writes Shirley R. Wolford, "and, as I remember it, the Canteen, with a few notable exceptions (I bow my head in shame for not remembering them), was serviced (except for entertainment) by the gals and guys of the lower echelons of the studios. Columbia's day was Thursday. . . ."

Another who remembers that side of the story is Betty Alnes of Redondo Beach. "I hate to destroy the nostalgic memories of millions of servicemen who poured through the Hollywood Canteen," she writes, "but I was one of the 'starlets' hostessing on Saturday nights. None of us was really in the movie industry directly.

"The fellows wanted so badly to dance with someone famous that we would tell them we were actresses. Since they had obviously never heard of us we'd weave stories that could put an old fisherman to shame. Saturday night was a busy night, so the boys came through in shifts of a half hour each. We got so that we could tell where a boy was from by the way he danced or talked. . . ."

The big-name people rarely showed up, Betty Alnes recalls, but some did, and some were loyal regulars. "Kay Kyser and his lovely wife Georgia were there every week, and Bette Davis, who was president, was always there—a beautiful, gracious lady. Mel Blanc bused tables all evening every week, but most of the other biggies put in token appearances. Some of our now famous actresses appeared on stage hoping to be spotted by agents.

"It was quite an education backstage, seeing who the gracious people were and who were actually opportunists. It was also the best place to pick up the latest Hollywood gossip. God, that place bred enough nostalgia to last a lifetime."

Marion Kaelin was a Lockheed secretary during the war and as a member of their Penguinettes Club she served at the Canteen as a hostess. She remembers it much as Betty Alnes does, but for Mrs. Kaelin the Canteen does have a romantic claim. It was there that she met her husband, but—well, it's her story.

"It was there," she recalls, "that Susan Hayward met Jess Barker, official M.C., when he leaned across her snack-bar station and said, 'Hey, why don't you and I get married or somethin'?' And she replied, 'We'll get married or *nothin'*.' They told us this at a shower for their twin boys. . . .

"Regulars were Bob Hope, Rudy Vallee and band, Bette

Davis, Angela Lansbury, Buddy Rich, who beat the drums in his Marine Corps uniform, Jack Benny, Bing Crosby, who worked with his corduroy-knickered sons, and James Melton, who sang with teen-ager Jane Powell. . . ."

As for Mrs. Kaelin's own story, it was at the Canteen that she met her future husband, Al, then in the Air Force, but it didn't "take" that time, as she puts it, and they had to meet twice more before it did.

"Four years later, at a UCLA Newman Club dance, we met again. That also dissolved. Three years later we met again at a local Bonaventure club party, and that time it took and is still in force, with a family of four in their twenties."

But Mrs. Kaelin didn't remember Al from the Canteen and would never have known that they had met that night if she hadn't been going through his wartime memoirs some years later and come across his boast that one night at the Canteen he had danced seven bars of "Mairzy Doats" with Shirley Temple.

"I knew that Shirley was there only once," says Mrs. Kaelin, "and I was there that time. Thus we reconstructed our one-hour Canteen friendship."

So the myth of the Canteen loses some of its luster. But you can't really knock a place that gave young Al Kaelin a preview of his wife-to-be and a chance to dance seven bars of "Mairzy Doats" with the future U.S. Ambassador to Ghana and provided the setting in which Miss Susan Hayward delivered, in real life, a line that so exquisitely encapsulated the Motion Picture Code that was shaping the morality of America:

"We'll get married or *nothin'!*"

18

The Eye of the Beholder

THE FAKE TOMATO FACTORY

"It's a place where cars live, and the people are just servants to keep the cars alive. . . ."

One of the unexpected bonuses I often find in current novels is the gratuitous paragraph about Los Angeles, usually a bleak little vignette thrown in when the author wants to make a comment about the crumminess, loneliness and emptiness of life in America.

It doesn't seem to matter where the hero or heroine happens to be at the moment, or how uncomfortable his situation; he simply conjures up a vision of Los Angeles and feels lucky to be where he is, by comparison.

The other evening I was reading *The Wind Chill Factor* by Thomas Gifford, where the hero goes back to his hometown, Cooper's Falls, Minnesota, during a blizzard in which the temperature falls to forty below zero, not to mention the wind-chill factor. Here he meets an old schoolmate, Paula, the town librarian, who has just come back from Los Angeles, a Vietnam widow. She had been married to a Los Angeles *Times* reporter, but he was killed in Laos.

"That was three years ago," she says, "and I stayed in L.A. for a while, working in a branch library, but, God, have you ever lived in California, John? It's some sort of updated Dantean inferno—highways, overpasses, underpasses, cars, cars, cars, sunshine, smog, the Dodgers and the Rams and the Lakers, drugs, and just unbelievable isolation."

She reflected for a moment, the author tells us, and flashed a nervous little smile. "Unbelievable," she goes on. "People do very peculiar things [in Los Angeles] because they're so insanely lonely. Things you're ashamed of afterward, things that eat away at your sanity when you think about them. . . ."

Evidently our Paula got involved in an orgy or two, which is of course what we all do in Los Angeles when we're overcome by the Dodgers and the Rams and the Lakers and that crazy loneliness, and it isn't really our fault, is it? It's this damn place.

Actually, it turns out that people do some very peculiar things in Cooper's Falls, too, even when the temperature is forty below. Paula herself is strangled by some mysterious visitor as she sits at her desk in the library, which is deserted because it's too cold for reading.

A day or two later I had switched locales, reading Walker Percy's new book, *Lancelot,* about an over-the-hill Louisiana football hero who idles the nights away in his remodeled pigeon loft, boozing and reading Raymond Chandler, while his movie-struck wife entertains the director of a Hollywood film company in her bed and his sixteen-year-old daughter entertains the male star and the female star, simultaneously, in hers.

Poor Lancelot, who ran a punt back 110 yards against Alabama and has never done anything that important since. Here he sits, drunk, cuckolded, confused, his Holy Grail forever beyond reach, while an emotional hurricane, coincident with the real one that is on its way, begins to tear at the wrappings of his life. But for the moment he is happy.

"The reason I was happy," he tells us, "was that I was reading for perhaps the fourth or fifth time a Raymond Chandler novel. It gave me pleasure. It was the only way I could stand my life, to sit there in old gold-green Louisiana under the levee and read, not about General Beauregard but about Philip Marlowe taking a bottle out of his desk drawer in his crummy office in seedy Los Angeles in 1933 and drinking alone and all those from-nowhere people living in stucco bungalows perched in Laurel Canyon. The only way I could stand my life in Louisiana, where I had everything, was to read about crummy lonesome Los Angeles in the 1930s. Maybe that should have told me something. If I was happy, it was an odd sort of happiness. But it was odder even than that. Things were split. I was physically in Louisiana but spiritually in Los Angeles. . . ."

We are used to reading about how lonely and desolate Los Angeles is. But I think maybe Percy has broken some ground here. He seems to be saying that no matter *where* a person is, if his life is crumbling, if he feels isolated and betrayed, if he has lost his sense of goal and worth, if he is just insanely lonely —then *spiritually* he is in Los Angeles.

I think it might become a popular metaphor, like saying someone is in Coventry. "Boy, am I in Los Angeles today!" Meaning, of course, that life doesn't seem worth living.

Of course Lancelot is drawn to Philip Marlowe by more than his locale. After all, he is a *failed* Lancelot, but Philip Marlowe was an uncorruptible Galahad, and though he knew there was no Holy Grail, too, he never stopped searching for it as if that legendary symbol of purity would be hiding in a place like Los Angeles.

Lancelot I think I understand. But Paula troubles me. Why should a nice young librarian with a job in a branch library in Los Angeles feel any more insanely isolated than the same librarian sitting alone at her desk in an empty library in Cooper's Falls in a blizzard?

Anyway, there's one consolation about living in Los Angeles. When you do get that feeling of insane isolation, at least you can always find something peculiar to do and some from-nowhere person to do it with.

Perhaps I am really onto something and not simply being paranoid in my notion that our current novelists feel almost obliged to throw in a couple of paragraphs about what a terrible place Los Angeles is.

Another fine example of the vogue is pointed out by a reader, Samuel Glasner, in a recent thriller called *The Domino Principle,* by Adam Kennedy.

Kennedy's philippic against our town runs to a page and a half and is delivered by a young woman named Thelma, who had tried to live here while her husband was in a Midwestern prison.

"I mean Los Angeles must have been a nice place once," she tells him after his escape, trying to break the news that she hadn't been faithful. "If it wasn't, all those people wouldn't have flocked out there, would they? But now . . . it makes you think it's a place where cars live and the people are just there as some kind of servants to keep the cars alive.

"It's hard to breathe there, too," she goes on. "I mean it. Some days there's a yellow cloud all the way from the ocean clear out to San Bernardino. Your eyes burn and water, and when you first go there you can't figure out what's wrong. Then they laugh and tell you it's just the smog. But it's not funny. It makes you think they'd laugh if somebody put rat poison in their coffee. I mean how can anybody be so crazy about living in a place that they love it even when it's terrible.

"The vegetables and the fruit don't taste good either. They're all fat and big and bright-colored, but when you put them in your mouth you can't tell what you're eating. A California tomato doesn't even taste like a tomato. It tastes like something that somebody invented or made in a fake tomato factory. When you eat anything that tastes good in California, you can bet it's shipped in. . . ."

We have to keep in mind that Thelma is trying to work up an explanation for why she cheated on her husband in Los Angeles, just as Paula, in *The Wind Chill Factor*, was trying to explain why she went to an orgy, or did whatever it was that made her feel ashamed afterward and ate away at her sanity.

Well, I was surprised and pleased the other day to receive an amiable letter from Gifford, the author of *The Wind Chill Factor*, and do you know where he lives now? Los Angeles.

"Let me rush to assure you," he says, "that all the 'Dantean Inferno' jazz about Los Angeles was poor, doomed little Paula talking—not me. The first time I was ever there—about two years ago, to meet with film producers—I was really smitten by the town. They . . . drove me all around the area, watched me gape at the rows of towering palms on Doheny . . . and we actually made a deal at the Polo Lounge . . . where they arranged to have me paged by the Phillip Morris fellow. The entire seduction took about four hours. A year later my wife, who is an actress, and I moved here and have enjoyed the whole thing immensely. . . . So forgive poor Paula. . . ."

I do; and I hope I made it clear that it was Paula talking, not necessarily the author.

Finding out that Gifford lived here, despite the quality of our tomatoes, I got to wondering where Kennedy lived, considering that his character, poor little Thelma, thought Los

Angeles was so ghastly. So I bought a copy of *The Domino Principle* and found what I was looking for at the back of the book.

"ABOUT THE AUTHOR. Adam Kennedy has been a professional painter, actor and screenwriter. A native of Indiana, he has lived in Paris and New York and is currently living in Beverly Hills. . . ."

I wonder how long it took them to seduce Adam Kennedy away from Indiana to our marvelous fake tomato factory.

Technically, of course, Beverly Hills is not Los Angeles. I imagine all their fruits and vegetables are imported, along with their wines, their clothes, their cars and the servants who keep their cars alive.

Even so, the air they breathe is pretty much the same air we breathe in Los Angeles, and the town is quite surrounded by Los Angeles; so even if you have a Beverly Hills address, geographically and spiritually you live in Los Angeles.

Meanwhile, if you want to see some really luscious tomatoes, just squeeze into the Polo Lounge some day about 5:00 P.M.

It is a rule of mine never to hurt or embarrass anyone merely for the sake of scoring a point or turning a clever phrase, so I am obliged to apologize to Adam Kennedy, author of *The Domino Principle*, for indicating that he lived in Los Angeles.

As I said, Beverly Hills is not technically Los Angeles, but it is surrounded by Los Angeles; and in essence, if you live in Beverly Hills you live in Los Angeles, though you may have a classier address. However, the point is academic, according to Kennedy himself, who writes as follows from an address on East Ninth Street in New York City:

"Regarding your May 3 column . . . it's true that in *The Domino Principle* I wrote some negative things about Los Angeles. It is not true that I live there. I have been a legal resident of New York City since 1961.

"My publishers are not sure where I live. I have been listed by them as resident in France, Portugal, Ireland, England *and* Beverly Hills, all partial truths. At various times. The fact is I tend to be homeless. . . .

"I have, however, spent a lot of time in Southern Califor-

nia. I have rented and leased and guested in Hollywood, Laurel
Canyon, Beverly Hills, Santa Monica, Malibu and Bel-Air. I've
had happy rewarding times there and I expect to have more in
the future. But I don't deceive myself that it's a place without
flaws, any more than New York is. Or Chicago. Or Indian-
apolis.

"I have no impulse, in other words, to hide behind Thelma
Tucker's skirts. Her views are *my* views. The air is unquestion-
ably polluted, people *are* enslaved by automobiles, and the
oranges and tomatoes do indeed leave a lot to be desired.
Especially if you want to eat them.

"*The Domino Principle* is my sixth novel. In the previous
five I had critical things to say about Paris, London, Berlin,
Mexico City, San Francisco, Miami, and Fort Benton, Mon-
tana. So Los Angeles is in good company. . . ."

I could say, on the contrary, that we were in *bad* company,
but that would be merely a trivial diversion from the point: To
state that a man who lives in New York City is actually a
resident of Los Angeles is libelous, on the face of it; and I hope
Mr. Kennedy will be satisfied by this retraction. I have no
impulse to hide behind the skirts of his publishers.

Also, I applaud Kennedy for refusing to hide behind
Thelma Tucker's skirts and for owning up to her opinions as
his own. Actually, I had discounted Mrs. Tucker's remarks,
considering her character. She is a real loser. She marries a
bank robber and murderer in an Indiana prison and comes out
to San Bernardino to wait for him, although he has to put in
twenty years before they'll even look at him for parole. Evidently she landed in Los Angeles before settling in San Bernardino and wasn't too happy with it.

Actually, I was willing to give her the benefit of the doubt.
You have to feel sorry for a woman who moves to San Bernardino to wait for an unregenerate sociopath who is doing hard
time in Indiana. I don't mean to knock San Bernardino, but of
course we who live in Los Angeles have to have some place to
feel superior to, the way people who live in New York City or
San Francisco feel superior to Los Angeles, and our place is San
Bernardino.

No contemporary novelist, by the way, can make Los Angeles look bleaker than Joan Didion can, but if you want to

read about a place that looks *really* bleak, catch her description of San Bernardino country in *Slouching Toward Bethlehem,* which is about a San Bernardino housewife who murdered her husband by setting fire to him in their Volkswagen. (That's the sort of thing they do out there, Ms. Didion suggests, on nights when their club isn't bowling.)

So, as I say, I would have blamed Mrs. Tucker's immoderate remarks on her mental state and the rather desolate outlook that her circumstances certainly seemed to warrant.

But if her appraisal of Los Angeles is Kennedy's too, it must be taken seriously, and if *The Fake Tomato Factory* catches on as the newest epithet for Los Angeles, and I think it's neat, he certainly will deserve the credit.

By the way, I don't want to give away the ending of *The Domino Principle,* but I imagine that, all things considered, Thelma Tucker would rather be living in Los Angeles.

LOS ANGELES THE MAGNIFICENT

"Professor Winters, like all lovers, is slightly mad."

Critics of Los Angeles, in the grand tradition, deplore our whole culture as a wasteland and specifically abominate our architecture as the lowest form of high kitsch. They disdain our dearest landmarks—from the Brown Derby restaurant to our Chinese theater—as symptoms of our general dementia, and our houses as comic crackerboxes inspired by the false-front fantasies of our movie lots.

Having had no schooling in architecture, I have always assumed they were right. But secretly I loved it all: our ancient Oriental theaters, our PWA Moderne and medieval schools, our Moorish garden courts, our Hansel and Gretel cottages, our French chateaux and Tudor mansions, our Gothic churches, our Assyrian rubber factory, our Zigzag Moderne department stores, our Spanish-Art Deco railroad depot, our wonderful Mediterranean-Roman-Hellenistic-Byzantine-Islamic-Egyptian-Goodhue library and our Beaux Arts-Byzantine-

Italian-Classic-Nebraska Modern City Hall with the Greek mausoleum of Halicarnassus on top.

For forty years I have admired most of these playful ornaments without knowing how to describe them in terms of architectural style. So I am happy to have at last *A Guide to Architecture in Los Angeles & Southern California*, by David Gebhard and Robert Winter. This is a monumental paperback, about the size and weight of a brick, and may be carried in a coat pocket while you explore the city, provided you carry a real brick in the opposite pocket as a counterbalance.

It was Winter, professor of history at Occidental College, who gave me a personal guided tour of the Victorian houses on Carroll Avenue a few years ago, and although the thousands of entries in this guide are necessarily terse, they radiate the professor's wit, exuberance and affection for Los Angeles, as well as his scholarship.

In a brilliant introduction the authors call Southern California "the most complete realization of the myth of the self-made, self-reliant, self-oriented individual the world has ever seen," but warn that our civilization is "fragile and tenuous," and we live dangerously at the end of our water lines. Photographs of an even dozen storied structures are scattered through the introductory text—a Greene and Greene house, the Carthay Circle, the Dodge House, the black and gold Richfield tower. Together, one realizes gradually, they constitute a graphic, wordless essay, because every one of the pictured objects has been destroyed.

I turned first to the pages on downtown Los Angeles and was pleased to find out not only that the old Eastern Columbia Building (Broadway at Ninth) is '20s Moderne in style but also that it is perfectly all right to like it. "Now that the black and gold Richfield building is gone, the Eastern Building assumes the mantle of being the major statement in L.A. of the '20s Moderne. It is clothed in light green terra-cotta with dark blue and gold trim. Its crowning glory is its large clock tower which is both Goodhue-esque and Gothic."

Even the stubby old forgotten office buildings on Spring Street, once thought to be about as high as a building orta go, are restored to dignity. For example, the Hibernian Building at 4th Street: "Often cited as L.A.'s first skyscraper, this 12-story

Beaux Arts office block exhibits an elaborately decorated attic with a row of Corinthian columns."

We are led over to Skid Row to admire the Pershing Hotel at Fifth and Main: "Another of the rare late nineteenth-century commercial buildings which is still around. As always, forget the first floor and look at the second floor of this brick building. Five classical decorated oriel bays and a corner bay tower punctuate the facade."

And we are brought back to the present by this note on the new Bonaventure Hotel: "The twenty-first century and Buck Rogers have not left us yet. A cluster of five bronze glass towers rising from their podium base—just like one of the drawings you can find on a 1940s cover of *Amazing Stories. . . .*"

But the real treasures are in our older residential districts. which are ornamented with landmark houses by such imaginative architects as Wright, Neutra, Schindler, Lautner and a dozen others who have approached the Southern California landscape with much the same vision and integrity. The guide lists hundreds of houses, some of which you perhaps have seen and wondered at in your own neighborhood; maps and addresses are given (with the injunction that viewers must respect the privacy of the tenants).

Naturally I was gratified to find a brief section devoted to my own neighborhood, Mt. Washington, and eagerly read the introductory note: "Mt. Washington—Artists' nests abound in this area above Highland Park and the 'real world.' It is said that Mt. Washington is above the smog. Not true. But it does, in spite of winding streets, give a sense of neighborhood as few places in Southern California do. Incidentally, we are sorry that Jack Smith's house cannot be viewed properly, and we have thus been forced to leave this storied structure out of the *Guide.* Perhaps it is best left to legend."

Oh well. It's better to be a legend than nothing. I wish they had listed it, though. I'd like to know what it is.

Saturday morning was homecoming day at Occidental College, and I drove up to that sylvan sanctuary in Eagle Rock to catch Dr. Winter's celebrated orientation lecture for newcomers, "Los Angeles the Magnificent."

Anyone who is new here, or who finds it hard to love Los

Angeles, should try to catch him next year. There is no match
for his eye, his wit and his fervor in eulogizing our strange city.

I had hoped to quote him at length, being a disciple of his.
But on scanning my notes, which I had scrawled in the dark as
he was showing slides, I realized that the words alone could
not suggest the force of Professor Winter's delivery.

His confession of love and hate for Los Angeles might
sound merely academic or perfunctory to a person denied the
passion of his voice and the astonishing virtuosity of his ges-
tures. On the dark side, his awe at the truly stupendous ugli-
ness of certain landmarks and the towering stupidity of certain
authorities could be fathomed only by one who saw him fall
down on the stage, literally, like a man divinely stricken.

Only an ironist can love Los Angeles, and at irony Professor Winter is unsurpassed. Words alone cannot conjure up the
laughter that echoes in his serious judgments, nor the serious
judgments in his laughter. Professor Winter is truly in love
with our exasperating city, and like all lovers he is slightly
mad.

"Los Angeles the *Magnificent!*" he began, like an apostle
revealing God to a crowd of skeptics. "I really *do* believe in
that title! . . . Many people have *sneered* at this city—particularly people from *Frisco!* . . ."

The lights dimmed, the slides came on. The pictures had
been taken by Professor Winter himself, though they were not
always as well framed and as sharply in focus as his opinions.
In his picture of the Million Dollar Theater and the Bradbury
Building I could see neither of those familiar objects; but it
didn't matter. As he pointed out, no one walking on Third and
Broadway ever sees them anyway.

"Most of the great decoration of the Million Dollar Theater is at the top," he said, "where no one ever looks. Of course
it will be the first thing to fall when we have the earthquake.
The *big* one. Oh, we live dangerously in Los Angeles—we have
no choice. It is our great existential challenge."

Of the Bradbury Building: He took a visitor into it once,
showing him the skylighted inner court with its marble and
cast-iron stairways and bird-cage elevators, and the friend was
shocked. "He said, 'Los Angeles doesn't *deserve* such a building!' "

He admonished his audience: I *demand* that you go down and see the Bradbury Building. It is one of our great creations."

Most of the slides had been put in the projector the wrong way, so the pictures were reversed, but it didn't matter. When you are looking at the County Mall, between the Music Center and the City Hall, it is no better one way than the other. "It is really one of the dumbest views in the world," said Professor Winter of that bleak wasteland of concrete and flagpoles. "It is essentially an underground parking lot, with a fountain on top, usually turned off, of course. It has that great, stupid, oafish unity you need in our society of law and order."

One of his slides was eloquent, looking up Fifth Street from the Biltmore to the Arco Tower, with the central library, quaint and vulnerable, in between. "When they built the Arco Tower they didn't realize what they were doing for the library. I hadn't especially liked it, but now, in between those other buildings, it's a little jewel. I hope it can be saved."

On freeways: "Without the freeways Los Angeles has no focus. You have got to *drive* to see the interesting things, and there are many of them. But everything you want to see is seventeen miles from everything else you want to see."

There was laughter, and perhaps a few tears, when he showed some of the wonders that are now gone—a real-estate office like a Sphinx; a sandwich stand like a rather obscene hot dog; an orange juice stand like an orange; and gone with those gimmicks, the black and gold Richfield Building ("One of the last great creations of Art Deco") and Occidental's fallen neighbor, Luther Burbank Junior High School ("The greatest monument to the pre-Columbian revival in the world, and they're tearing it down").

Finally, the Watts Towers, Simon Rodia's marvelous gift to the people of Los Angeles. "Simon Rodia said, 'I wanted to do something big—and I did!' That should be on the Great Seal of the City of Los Angeles. *'I wanted to do something big—and I did.'*"

In the 1950s, Professor Winter recalled, the city wanted to pull the towers down, but to quiet the protests, they agreed to put them to a test of a 30,000-pound pull. If they stood the test, they would be spared. They stood the test.

"That proved," said Professor Winter, "that there is a God."

LEO POLITI

"He lived in a bower at Echo Park and came out only in the morning, with the dew."

Several times over the past few years, on days that invited it, I have walked or taken the minibus over to the Plaza to remind myself that Los Angeles had a pastoral beginning and was not created overnight by some dreadful Southern Pacific train wreck.

If it was not too hot I would have lunch at a cafe on Olvera Street and then look in on the mural that Leo Politi was painting across the front of the Biscailuz Building, which faces the Plaza to the east of Olvera Street and houses the Mexican Consulate.

I never once saw Politi at work. Instead of being painted, the mural seemed to be emerging of its own volition according to some exquisitely slow time scheme, like a picture puzzle whose pieces had been hidden and were being put in place as each was found.

It was to be a painting of the blessing of the animals, an ancient event that is reenacted each year on the Plaza. One day it would look as if a dog had been added, and a week or two later a goat, and then a child, or a white dove flying in a new patch of sky.

I might have doubted that there really was a Leo Politi, but I had the evidence in my own library at home—his book of words and paintings on our city's older parks and another on the exuberant old houses of Bunker Hill, now gone, along with the hill itself. There were also in existence a dozen other books, known to most schoolchildren, I hope, such as *Little Pancho* and *Pedro, the Angel of Olvera Street.*

But in thirty years as a newspaperman in a city whose religion is publicity, I had rarely seen Politi's name in the papers, and I had seen him in person only once, when a mutual friend kidnaped him, from wherever he hides out, and introduced us over lunch. I recall that Politi avoided excessive conversation on that occasion by sketching me and our friend on his menu. I fancied then that he lived in a bower at Echo Park and came out only in the morning, with the dew, to commune with birds and butterflies and children on their way to school.

Then finally the mural was finished, and I went over to the Plaza the other day for the dedication. It had been raining hard that morning, but it stopped just before the ceremonies began, and the red cap and cape of Cardinal Manning seemed fluorescent under the bright clouds.

"It's a miracle, the rain is stopping," said a woman standing next to me.

"I don't know," I said, "but it's certainly nice."

Politi himself was there: gaunt, sinewy, grizzled, slightly stooped, but with large eyes that seem always full of wonder. It was a face that might have been painted by El Greco.

The material costs of the mural had been paid by a foundation set up by her father in memory of Filippa Pollia, a joyous child who died suddenly in 1936 at the age of eight. Politi gave his time and talent, and it was a mating of spirits that transcended the temporal problems which sometimes intruded.

The people in Politi's mural looked gentle, innocent, serene. The white-haired man playing a violin; the young woman with a dog in her arms; the children leading their pets; the priest sprinkling the animals with holy water. It seemed sadly ironic that this peaceful scene could have been painted in the same century as Pablo Picasso's "Guernica," with its people and animals perishing in horror. But of course all our centuries show both sides of our coin.

There are those who would say Politi's mural is not real —that there is no gentleness, innocence, serenity or beauty left. But of course there are such things. They are in the eye of the beholder, and Leo Politi is our beholder.

"The harp player was a blind musician who used to be on Olvera Street," he said. "The old man playing the violin also played music on the street about that time. He was a thin and tall and handsome old man. The young lady with the white poodle in her arms works in a booth on Olvera Street. The baby in the basket on the donkey's back is a baby I saw in the arms of her mother sitting on a bench across the street. I sketched the little sparrows when they came on quieter days to feed on the pavement at the foot of the mural. The two dogs playing under the stairway are my dogs, Emmet and Oscar."

After all the speeches, Cardinal Manning said a prayer and then walked along Politi's painting, sprinkling holy water on his people and their creatures, and the Sheridan Street School band, which had been waiting through all the ceremony like a gathering storm, burst forth with extraordinary bravura and panache. I may not know anything about art, but I played clarinet one year in junior high school, and I know something about school bands. Believe me, that Sheridan gang is great.

I doubt if the Biscailuz Building was constructed to last for centuries, like Notre Dame, but if it does, people may look at Politi's mural a thousand years from now and see that there were gentle people once upon a time in Los Angeles, or anyway there was a Leo Politi.

RIGHT ON RED

"Next in importance to drive-in churches . . . I would place the Frisbee."

Now that *Annie Hall* has won an Oscar as the best movie of the year, its audience will be increased by millions, I imagine, and one of its clever insights into the culture of Los Angeles will be that much more widespread.

There is a line of dialogue in the film in which Woody Allen says, "What can you say about a place whose main contribution to culture is that you can turn right on a red light?" (Those may not be the exact words, but I don't want to get into another tempest like the one over the last line of *Casablanca*.)

Not only did Woody Allen's line reach millions who had already seen *Annie Hall*, but it was brought into the consciousness of many millions more over television on the night of the Academy Awards when Marshall Brickman, co-author of the movie, repeated it in accepting the Oscar for best original screenplay.

Thus, we have one more feather in our cap. Smogville, the Nowhere City, Moronia, Forty Suburbs in Search of a City, the Fake Tomato Factory will also be known throughout the world now as the place whose main contribution to culture is the right turn on a red light.

Woody Allen has already won enough plaudits for *Annie Hall*, but it would be churlish of us not to thank him for adding to the catalogue of insults that are such a rich and enjoyable part of our legend.

I'm not sure, though, that Woody Allen and his co-author didn't overlook some of our other major innovations in singling out the right turn on a red light as our main contribution to culture.

If I'm not mistaken it was here in Los Angeles, or in one of our forty searching suburbs, that the first drive-in church appeared. This extraordinary invention is generally overlooked, I believe, when the cultural contributions of Los Angeles are enumerated and appraised.

One can say a great deal for the Second Vatican Council, the discovery of the Dead Sea Scrolls, the Billy Graham Crusades and the Jesus Movement, but I suspect that the drive-in church will be seen from the perspective of history as the greatest spur to the mid-twentieth-century revival of Christianity. (It may be that other faiths besides the Christian also have drive-in temples of worship, but I rather doubt it, as we Christians own most of the cars.)

I don't know whether we actually pioneered the drive-in bank also, but obviously it was an inevitable extension of the drive-in church, and if it happened to turn up first in some place like Good Thunder, Minnesota, you can bet they got the idea from us. Once it was demonstrated that we could do business with God without getting out of our automobiles, there was no reason to believe we couldn't also do business that way with Mammon.

Next in importance to drive-in churches and right turns on the red light, measured by their ultimate significance in Western civilization, I would place the Frisbee. This simple but astonishingly versatile aircraft—for that is what it is—was also invented right here in Los Angeles by a city building inspector named Walter F. Morrison.

That was back in 1949, but it wasn't until 1957, when a man from Wham-O saw Morrison playing with one of his flying saucers at the County Fairgrounds, that the Frisbee was born. Wham-O, it may be remembered, was the San Gabriel toy company that loosed the Hula Hoop craze on the nation, and while it cannot be stated that we invented the Hula Hoop here in Los Angeles, we certainly were the first to recognize its cultural potential and the first to make it available to society at large.

Of course the principle of the Hula Hoop had long been understood. When I was a boy I used to know a girl named Lucille who could do things with a barrel hoop that I have rarely seen the likes of since, even on the runway. But it took the amiable climate of Southern California to nourish the idea of turning the barrel hoop into a larger plastic ring and mass producing it in pretty colors. Overnight, millions of cultists were sent into their tireless gyrations.

There may be some argument, too, that the Frisbee is not purely a native contribution. At the time Wham-O bought the patent from Morrison, it is said, there was a bakery in New England named Frisbee, and its pie tins were being used by college students in the neighborhood for catch and other games. Thus, the name Frisbee. But once again, it was the vision, genius and energy of Los Angeles that made the Frisbee not just a pickup plaything but an international phenomenon which, like the Seven Seas, has washed up on the beaches of every civilized nation in the world.

I'm sure that if I put my mind to it I could remember numerous other cultural contributions made by Los Angeles and environs, including the doggie bag, which I believe was first offered to its patrons by a steak house in the San Fernando Valley.

For the time being, though, perhaps we should be content with the credit we have received in 1977's very best movie and the knowledge that someday the whole world will be turning right on a red light, except in England, of course, where it wouldn't work.

LETTER FROM LOS ANGELES

"So there we were, Marvin and I, in the Jacuzzi. . . ."

From time to time here I have noted with alarm what I thought was a decline in the frequency and intensity of journalistic putdowns of Los Angeles, but I no sooner begin to worry about it than a new one comes along.

I am sometimes accused of aiding and abetting such critics by collecting and broadcasting their pieces. "I sometimes think," writes G. Merle Bergman, "that you are helping to create the myth that everybody hates Los Angeles. . . . I wish the detractors and those like yourself who pay attention to the detractors would go to wherever it is you think beauty lies and leave this magnificent city to the rest of us who can love it without feeling any need to apologize."

It chagrins me that Bergman can imagine I have ever seriously apologized for Los Angeles or that I would prefer to live somewhere else. I'm sure there are more beautiful places, and better places to live, but not for me. However, all the purple prose ever written about palm trees, sunsets and snow-capped mountains doesn't get as close to defining the qualities that make Los Angeles wonderful as the tantrums of the critics it inspires.

I love and collect such essays because I think they're funny. They make me laugh, the way we used to laugh at Edgar Kennedy when he was angry. I like to think they make all of us laugh, except the most thin-skinned chauvinists. And our capacity for laughing at our critics, and at ourselves, instead of sulking and rushing to our mirrors for reassurance, like San Franciscans, is one of the reasons I prefer to live here than in Leningrad, which is thought to be more pleasing to the cultured eye, or in Oakland, which, year in year out, has a better football team.

As I say, I would miss these periodical defamations of our character and style if the supply were suddenly to dry up; but fortunately there seems to be no bottom to the well.

The latest to come my way is a "Letter from Los Angeles" by one Marcelle Clements, written to her fellow expatriates in Paris, evidently, and published in the English-language *Paris Métro.* Miss Clements not only has a wicked style, reminiscent of the most dyspeptic French *feuilletonists,* but also seems to write, in this case, from a sense of moral and physical debasement, or at least a near miss, Los Angeles in her eye being not only ugly and debilitating but spiritually dangerous as well.

"Descartes, where are you when I need you?" she begins. "I can't believe that no one ever warned me that traveling from Paris straight to Los Angeles is a perilous spiritual stunt to be attempted only by those who are impervious to nefarious attacks of culture shock. . . .

"I tried, I really did try to like Los Angeles," she goes on. "I dutifully gorged myself with tacos, sunshine, and *New West* magazine, I stood by without flinching while grown people used 'Catch you later' as a parting salutation. I milled fearlessly at film premieres, my poor little Parisian dress a pale blot in the panorama of tassels, paillettes, and leather thongs. . . . I struggled to endow L.A. with the poetic image of an amusing vulgar garden of eerie, tawdry blooms. I even tried telling myself 'It's so bad it's good.'

"I must admit defeat. Nothing about Parisian life equips human beings for this sort of thing. It's a leap into the time warp. But is this the city of the future? O brave new world!"

Miss Clements' most repulsive experience seems to have been a bath in a whirlpool tub with a chap named Marvin. "So there we were, Marvin and I, in the Jacuzzi, and I tried desperately to enjoy the bountiful (glaring) California sun, the warm undulations of water stroking my (chlorine soaked) limbs. I attempted to gaze dreamily upon nature; stray little droplets, for example, shimmering on Marvin's droopy mustache and in the folds of his tanned jowls, slip-sliding in sweet little rivulets down his tanned half-immersed pot belly. I don't know what's wrong with me. Somehow, I just couldn't . . . enjoy . . ."

Miss Clements also found that the only subjects of conversation in Los Angeles were automobiles, power and money. I think she overlooked sex, busing and the Dodgers, but perhaps she didn't get in with the intellectual crowd.

She says Woody Allen was "quite right" when he observed that the "main cultural advantage [in Los Angeles] is making a right turn on a red light." Miss Clements' use of Allen's quip shows that it has already become a cliché and is destined to become a classic.

"So you can't really blame me, can you," Miss Clements asks her Parisian friends, "if I pine for Les Halles? Give me the past, any day, because the future, viewed from here, is just too melancholy. . . ."

I wonder, though, if Miss Clements might have been less melancholy if the luck of the draw had put her into a tub with a rather more palatable partner than the feckless Marvin.

I am at your service, Miss Clements. Catch you later?

19

Seeing Stars

THE DIVINE SARAH AND FRIENDS

"For God's sake don't bend over—you'll close the show!"

It is commonly accepted as historical fact that Los Angeles was without culture in the 1920s and '30s except for movies, roller skating, Aimee McPherson, USC football and the Main Street Gym.

Now and then, though, I receive a letter from some resident of that era who insists there were legitimate theaters here and a fairly respectable theatrical tradition. Though these ramblings often seem to be refracted by the prism of time, I have discovered, by looking through the theater ads in newspapers of those days, that they are not entirely hallucinatory.

In an outpouring of nostalgia, for example, Robert Shillaker recalls that when he came to Los Angeles in the mid-1920s the Majestic and the Morosco were open on Broadway, and the old Mason Opera House was soon to be refurbished for *Seventh Heaven,* the romantic play that later became one of the most beloved of motion pictures and made stars of Janet Gaynor and Charles Farrell.

Then came *No, No, Nanette,* he recalls, which surprised everyone by running eight months. Up until then, everyone thought the only kind of theater that would play in Los Angeles was something inspirational, such as Mrs. McPherson or *The Pilgrimage Play.*

"The cast was so exactly right for the story," Shillaker remembers. "Taylor Holmes as Jimmy Smith and Nancy Welford in the title role. I wonder whatever happened to Marie Wells. . . .

"Grand opera and light opera were presented annually at the old Philharmonic (actually the Temple Baptist Church). I remember John Charles Thomas in *Blossom Time,* and this is where I first heard Lawrence Tibbett and Nelson Eddy.

"Just before the start of the Depression, or at least before it got bad out here, there was a spate of new theater buildings: three in Hollywood—the El Capitan, the Vine Street and the Playhouse, which was later to house Ken Murray's *Blackbirds.* Remember when Marie Wilson did her ladylike striptease down to her lingerie, causing—in those days—an audible gasp from the audience?"

It was Ken Murray's *Blackouts,* not *Blackbirds.* I remember that myself. Also, I can say for Miss Wilson that if she were to strip down to her lingerie onstage today there would still be an audible gasp—if only from me. Miss Wilson would make two of Farrah Fawcett-Majors, and not an ounce too much.

"The El Capitan was the perfect intimate theater," Shillaker continues. "Spanish in style. Many were the enjoyable evenings I spent at the El Capitan. I remember particularly Sidney Kingsley's *Men in White.* But most of all *Parnell.* Coming out of the theater with a friend, neither of us said a word. We walked two blocks in the wrong direction before we returned to earth. . . .

"Shortly after, two new theaters opened near Eleventh and Hill, a funny place to locate a theater. One wonders where would have been the right location. But they did well for a few years. People still used to ride the Big Red Cars in 1930 and you weren't afraid to be out at night, even alone. The Mayan achieved a notable success with *Grand Hotel.* After the scene in the third act where the industrialist's secretary is forced to disrobe down to stockings and teddy, I remember my date saying, 'They didn't have to go that far!' But Tallulah Bankhead had already done it, and in staid London, too. . . ."

Ah, Tallulah! She was a caution; a woman before her time. I wonder if Shillaker happened to read the story we had in the *Times* a week or two ago in which friends of the late Tallulah reminisced about her fondly, one paragraph reading exactly as follows:

"Bankhead's lack of inhibition was legendary, and Miss Kelly (actress Patsy Kelly) recalled that when Miss Bankhead greeted a plumber wearing only a very short cashmere sweater, she asked the startled man, 'What's the matter? Haven't you ever seen a cashmere sweater before?' "

Oddly, two or three readers clipped that paragraph and sent it to me, though I wasn't its author. They seemed to question the syntax, saying it left some doubt whether it was Miss Bankhead who was wearing the cashmere sweater, or the plumber. Of course that complaint is frivolous. True, the first part of the sentence may be ambiguous, but Miss Bankhead's remark to the plumber makes it plain that she, not he, was so attired.

Besides, if it had been the plumber who wore only the sweater, it is almost certain that Miss Bankhead, who was a very poised as well as uninhibited woman, would have said, "Well, my good man, I'm happy to see that at least you haven't forgotten your tools."

Shillaker recalls seeing Lionel Barrymore and Joe E. Brown at the Belasco in *Laugh Clown Laugh,* Ruth Chatterton in *The Vinegar Tree* and Basil Rathbone in *The Command to Love,* in which Rathbone delivered the memorable line: "I may have deceived the ladies. I have never disappointed them."

I offer Shillaker's memories simply as memories, not as facts. But I happen to believe him, and I wish I knew what happened to Marie Wells.

Robert Shillaker's recollections have been echoed by numerous other readers who recall a time when they could take a streetcar downtown and see anything from Minsky's burlesque at the Temple Baptist Church to a one-legged Sarah Bernhardt playing the title role in *Camille* without getting out of bed.

Maybe it wasn't the Great White Way, but it must have been fun.

George and Virginia Cook of Santa Ana recall a production of *The Gorilla* at the Morosco "where an actor in a gorilla suit terrorized the audience by running up and down the aisles. . . ."

In those days audiences weren't inured to violence as they are today by the nightly slaughter on TV, and the Cooks still remember the thrill of a blank cartridge being fired onstage and "the horrible hand emerging from the woodwork toward the innocent heroine."

"Your column . . . almost drowned me in a wave of nostalgia," writes Una M. French of Alhambra. "I saw all those plays and more. I remember Basil Rathbone's famous line. He was about to leave the stage, almost running, and unbuttoning his coat as he ran. I think the woman who was waiting for him was Mary Nash. . . .

"We saw Ken Murray's *Blackouts* often. Once in a scene with Marie Wilson I remember his saying: 'For God's sake don't bend over—you'll close the show!' "

"I fondly recall," writes Leo Simon, once a fellow scribbler on the *Daily News*, "sitting up in the last row top balcony with my Jefferson High School drama class at the old Mason Opera house on Broadway drinking in every word of Walter Hampden as Cyrano.

"No question," he adds, agreeing with me, "that Marie Wilson's ample charms and comedic talent would elicit an audible sigh from an audience today. I remember reviewing *Blackouts* for our alma mater, and enjoying every little thing she did and said." Ah, yes, Leo—every little movement had a meaning all its own.

Sarah Bernhardt's recumbent Camille is recalled by Ormond K. Flood of Whittier. "She had had her leg amputated and did it (the play) entirely in bed. Afterward she took her curtain calls standing behind a chair. The applause was great. Pour soul. She was terribly in debt and trying to raise a little money."

"I was a member of the cast of *No, No, Nanette*," writes Mrs. W. F. Coates of Malibu, "along with Nancy Welford, Taylor Holmes, Tyler Brooks and Mia Martin. I was Dorothy Whitmore. . . ."

Robert Shillaker saw that show, too, and wondered what had happened to Marie Wells.

"Marie Wells was one of my good friends," says Mrs. Coates. "a beautiful girl, with a beautiful voice and loads of talent. I believe she later starred with Perry Askam in *The Desert Song*. They were very much in love. . . ."

"Marie Wells died in 1949 at the age of fifty-five," writes Edwin L. Brooks. "I guess Mr. Shillaker wanted to know."

"The Orpheum was a vaudeville house," recalls Carroll Shepphird of Newport Beach, "presenting such greats as Jack Benny, Ted Lewis, the Marx Brothers, Fred Waring, Hobard Bosworth, Toto the Clown and many others including dog acts. The dog acts were always last.

"The Mayan opened in the late '20s and I remember Fredric March playing John B. in a great play, *The Royal Family*. My wife and I, in our best clothes, took the yellow car which ran by the theatre from our apartment several miles away. . . ."

Charles Leonard of Laguna Hills recalls another important downtown theater—the Playhouse in the Friday Morning Club on Figueroa. "I remember because I helped Louis McLoon, a former Broadway press agent pal, open the house with the great Doris Keane (of *The Czarina* fame) in that marvelous heart crusher, *Romance.* I can still hear her declaim that famous curtain line: 'Open your heart and let God in!'

"But I remember the job because Louis paid me $35 a week ('half in salary and half in climate' were his hiring words), and I was compelled to take it because I had come to L.A. broke and was sharing a furnished apartment with Jimmy and Billy Cagney on nearby Arapahoe Street off Washington. If you want more, you'll have to buy my lunch—or I yours."

I might accept the invitation, but Leonard will have to buy. Half of my pay is in climate.

PROGRAM FOR THE ORPHEUM

"It sounds like an age of elegance and sophistication."

Ormond Flood's recollection of seeing Sarah Bernhardt play the title role in *Camille* entirely in bed was so graphic, with Miss Bernhardt leaning on a chair to take her curtain calls, that I accepted it without question, only to receive this note from John T. Quinlan of La Jolla.

"It was *L'Aiglon*, not *Camille*, Mr. Smith. But keep hanging in there. Maybe some day you will get things straight."

Checking it out seemed too formidable a job of research, perhaps with long hours spent at the library going through old newspapers. But a piece of evidence partly supporting Flood came from another reader, Allen Pollock, who sent me an original souvenir program of the appearance of Miss Bernhardt and her company in repertory at the Orpheum.

It was the program for the second week of the company's two-week engagement here, and it noted that Miss Bernhardt herself would appear as the empress in *Théodora*, as Marion la Vivandière in *Une Nuit de Noël sous la Terreur* and as Marguerite Gautier in *La Dame Aux Camélias*, or, as she is known in America, Camille. Orchestra seats were $1; boxes and loges $1.50; balcony 50 and 75 cents; family circle 50 cents and gallery 10 cents. Just to make sure of an audience, I suppose, there was also a vaudeville bill.

The program is undated, and I can only guess, from the advertisements, that the company was here in the spring of 1913. So this may not have been the *Camille* that Flood saw, since it was not until 1915 that Miss Bernhardt lost her leg, but at least it appears to prove that she did play Camille here.

But the ads in the program tell us something about the quality of life in that era here, almost better than any other medium could. The James B. Forbes Co. was advertising a new tract called Michillinda. "The Showplace of Huntington Drive," offering "little half acre estates in a large, beautifully improved private park, thirty minutes out, at $1,155 per half acre. . . ."

Nelson's, 434 South Broadway, was describing its new spring line of men's clothing as "more snappy than ever. . . . Beautiful English garments, slightly form-fitting. Natural shoulders and soft roll lapels. High cut waistcoats with or without collar. Straight English cut trousers. Every little detail about our garments is right up to the minute. . . ."

A full-page ad for Orange Blossom candies was illustrated with a drawing of a gentleman in top hat and tails waiting for a lady with rolled stockings to finish putting on her makeup. Underneath the drawing was this snappy repartee:

"Instead of sending me flowers, why don't you bring me orange blossoms once in a while?"

"Er—I say—aren't orange blossoms flowers?"

"I mean Orange Blossom Candy, stupid!"

The Corenson Hair Co., 619½ South Broadway (opposite

the Orpheum), offered real human hair in a cluster of thirty to forty puffs, "soft and lustrous," for fifty-nine cents. "Come across the street to the house that guarantees their hair goods."

The Cawston Ostrich Farm store, 313 South Broadway, offered "the matchless beauty and superior quality of Cawston Plumes, the result of twenty-six years of scientific ostrich feather culture and production."

Newcomb's Corset Shop, 533 South Broadway, offered the improved front-laced corset which, when properly fitted, "is comfortable from the moment it is put on."

Half a page is devoted to spring fashion notes for women. "The skirt for the coming season is the delightful walking width of two yards, though we still have the yard and a half width. Instead of the hobble skirt this season we have the plait. . . ."

And after the show, smart theatergoers would be seen at the Cafe Bristol, which occupied the entire basement of the H. W. Hellman building, Fourth and Spring, the Black Cat in the Hotel Hayward, Sixth and Broadway, or the Echo Tavern, 449 South Spring.

A two-page directory of automobile dealers extolled the merits of such models as Velie, Pathfinder, Simplex and Mercer, and the Borland Electric Co., 830 South Broadway, had a page of its own, advertising "from Chicago to Milwaukee on a single charge—a distance of 104 miles through sand and mud. . . ."

It sounds like an age of elegance and sophistication, except for that Orange Blossom ad and maybe one other. Making capital of Miss Bernhardt's age, which would have been sixty-eight in 1913, Berman's Trunk Factory advertised that "the wonderful lasting qualities of the Divine Sarah we find again in Berman's luggage. . . ."

It must have amused the gallant lady, near the end of her distinguished career, to be in Los Angeles and find herself described in print as a piece of baggage.

JOAN CRAWFORD

*"She was the first woman I had ever seen
in her teddies."*

Joan Crawford died rich and famous the other day in her East Side Manhattan apartment, which is pretty good for a girl who started out as a Kansas City hoofer, and her obituary needs no amplification from me.

But Joan Crawford was my kind of movie star, and I would hate to think that I had held back something that might add even one candlelight to the flame of her memory.

I didn't know Miss Crawford, except from her movies and the tons of slush we wrote about her over the past fifty years; but I met her once, in person, privately, just the two of us, and I am not likely ever to forget it.

I was a reporter at the time and had been sent out to 20th Century–Fox to interview the lady. I was never of the breed we call Hollywood reporters, and to this day I don't know anyone in the industry above the rank of press agent, although I had lunch once with Henry Wilcoxon, and Keenan Wynn calls me now and then on the telephone.

So I was hardly less agitated than a regular reader of *Screen Romances* might have been as I waited for Miss Crawford in the small entry of her dressing room. It was not simply a room, of course, but rather a large suite, elegantly furnished to the taste of one of those fussy French kings and in keeping with Miss Crawford's stature as a star of the first magnitude.

Our files tell me that this interview took place in the spring of 1959, shortly after the death of her fourth husband, who had been chairman of the board of Pepsi-Cola. Miss Crawford had come back to Fox, after an absence of seven years, to play a rather small role as a career woman in *The Best of Everything,* but she had recently been elected to the board of Pepsi-Cola herself, and it was to elicit her reflections on that career, evidently, that I had been sent.

Miss Crawford would then have been fifty-one years old,

and certainly I was old enough and professional enough, I would have thought, to keep the lady in focus simply as the subject of what was likely to be a rather dry interview, however much Pepsi she managed to pour into it.

But as I say, Joan Crawford had always been my kind of movie star, and as I waited to be fetched into her presence my concentration gave way to feverish images. I had been but a small boy when she starred in *Our Dancing Daughters,* but one of its scenes still flashed white hot on some private screen in my mind. It was Miss Crawford dancing the Charleston in her teddies. She would have been twenty then, about the age of my sister, and I suppose she was the first woman I had ever seen in her teddies, except my sister, and of course one didn't count one's sister.

The door to Miss Crawford's chamber was slightly ajar, and I could hear the voices of two women, indistinctly. In a while one of them came out, leaving the door ajar, and left, giving me a noncommittal nod. Minutes went by. Had Miss Crawford forgotten me? Should I knock?

A bare foot appeared in the crack of the doorway. It swept the door back and was followed into the open doorway by the full figure of its owner—a very handsome woman in a pale blue slip. She was slightly crouched, holding a tray of dirty coffee dishes which she evidently meant to place on a low table by my chair. There was a cigarette, unlighted, protruding from the exact center of her mouth. She saw me. Her motion stopped. She stood staring at me from her strange crouch, tray in hand. She was speechless, of course, because of the cigarette in her mouth. But her eyes were eloquent! Those marvelous dark eyes like dark islands in flashing seas of white. Now they were full of astonishment. The astonishment gave way to embarrassment and embarrassment to humor. The cigarette fell from her lips to the tray.

"Hello," she said.

I stood. "Miss Crawford, I presume."

I know this incident will seem utterly banal to some of my friends who work the Hollywood scene and consider it routine to interview actresses in their baths and in fact find it difficult to escape their beds, to hear them tell it; but it must be kept in mind that for the moment, as we confronted each other in that little foyer, I was an innocent boy again, and Miss Crawford was the first woman I had ever seen in teddies, except my sister.

A week or two later I received a note from Miss Crawford on pale-blue stationery. I have kept it:

MY DEAR JACK:
This is just to say thank you again for the wonderful article you wrote on me. I'm so deeply grateful to you. No wonder people like you so much. You really quote them accurately, which is a rarity these days. Bless you, and I hope to see you soon to thank you personally.

JOAN

It is naturally my practice, when quoting from letters, to delete any lines of praise, however great the temptation to give them a wider audience. I beg the reader's indulgence for departing from that rule in this case. I simply want to show that, in my accounts, Joan Crawford was a very gracious lady.

CENSORED GOODS

"They did it with their clothes on, and they did it sober."

People who long for the restoration of censorship over books and movies, being nauseated, they say, by too much sex and violence, may be too young to have seen what censorship was like, or too old to remember.

I don't mean political censorship, which thanks to the Founding Fathers we have generally been spared in America, but the censorship, on moral grounds, of words and pictures, which goes back to our Puritan forebears and seeks to protect us from our baser yearnings.

Even for those of us who remember, it is hard to believe that only two or three decades ago *Lady Chatterley's Lover*, *Ulysses* and *Tropic of Cancer* were routinely seized by U.S. Customs agents, along with opium, as unfit for American consumption.

It is even harder to remember that in the 1920s and 1930s
every American-made movie we saw had either been censored
by the Hays Office or filmed with meek obeisance to the Hays
Office Code to escape its scissors. We loved the movies, and if
the world they showed us was strangely bare of manners and
morals that even a child couldn't help observing, that was part
of the wonderful illusion.

In those days I was too young and innocent to know that
I was watching censored goods, and besides, the great themes
were not entirely disallowed. Women might still fall from vir-
tue (how many other kinds of stories are there?) but they did it
with their clothes on, for all I could see, and during Prohibition
they did it sober.

I never knew the mechanics of the system, though, until
the other day when a friend sent me a copy of some correspon-
dence in 1926 between Will Hays, the censor, Jesse Lasky, the
studio chief, and Julian Johnson, who was Lasky's producer on
a silent version of *The Great Gatsby.*

Evidently the transgressions of *The Great Gatsby* were so
flagrant that Mr. Hays got Mr. Lasky on the long-distance telephone, as it was called then, and told him to hold everything,
letter follows.

In the letter, which refers to that conversation, Hays reminded Lasky that the Code allowed neither scenes nor titles
(this was before sound) reflecting the "slightest" disregard for
the law, which of course included Prohibition. Drinking could
not be shown or mentioned, unless it was essential to the plot
or the development of character, presumably character in decline.

I can't remember seeing that early *Gatsby.* I would have
been a small boy, anyway, and might not have suspected what
had been cut out. But here, in Hays's own words, is what I
would have missed. He told Lasky:

> You will notice when you review it, the scene of Miss
> Wilson in bed in negligee getting drunk, the interior
> scenes of girls in one-piece bathing suits running around
> the house drinking; the scene of the man and the girl on
> the float in the pool kissing; the scene of trays and more
> trays of cocktails on the table and on the water; the scenes
> of the drunken girls in the shower bath; the wind blowing

the two women's skirts; the scene in the apartment where a conductor and the woman are drunk; the scene of Miss Wilson's husband and another man's wife at various stages, particularly the woman's dress. . . .

Well, I would have guessed that Lasky, who presumably had read the book, would have written Hays back, at once, saying something like, "What the hell are you talking about, Hays? If you take booze and sex out of *The Great Gatsby* you haven't got anything left!"

But evidently Lasky hadn't read the book. He simply called his man Johnson and gave him the word, because the next letter is from Johnson to Lasky, and it's a complete cop-out: The bloody work had been done, he reported, like Queen Elizabeth's ministers reporting that Mary's head was safely off.

Specifically, he noted, he had cut the following:

Scene of bathing girls under shower, drinking, and who also appear to be drunk.

One of the flashes in the closeup of the wind blowing dresses of Daisy and Jordan Baker.

Scenes of bathing girls in the room where they speak the titles: "Here's to Gatsby! . . . Who's Gatsby? . . . Nobody knows. . . . Nobody cares. . . ."

I offer a salute, long overdue, to the author of that last scene, so wantonly aborted. Without sound, with nothing but a handful of words flashed at the bottom of the screen, he or she had brilliantly caught the mystery and loneliness of Gatsby and the mood of that gaudy summer at Gatsby's place.

Alas, those words, like so many other works of art, had fallen to the cutting-room floor, and their author, no doubt, like so many of his colleagues, had taken to bootleg drinking in despair.

Soon enough we will have had our fill of blood and naked sex in our movies, and restraint will set in. But let's don't have the censors back. I kind of like to see women's dresses blowing in the wind.

20

L.A. Going...Going...

PALOVERDE

*"Love," she sighs with melancholy resignation. "Love is
why I must live here."*

Since it is widely supposed that Los Angeles had no history but was simply erected overnight, about 1926, by Republic
Studios, we can hardly wonder that there have been so few
historical romances with a Los Angeles setting.

Not only is there no history, according to the conventional
wisdom, but there is no romance, and it is assumed that *The
Day of the Locust,* which Nathanael West wrote in 1938, in
the last throes of the Great Depression, is the definitive comment on our culture, brilliantly depicting its falsity, shallow-
ness, madness and vulgarity.

Given this lackluster and repulsive reputation, Los Angeles of course has not inspired the lusty romances that arise
from San Francisco like the night fogs, nor can we hope that
James Michener will discover our history some day and peel it
away, layer after layer, until at last we make the best-seller
list.

This being so, I have all the more admiration for Jacque-
line Briskin, a local girl who made good, for daring to write
Paloverde, a novel with a Los Angeles background, in the grand
tradition of historical family sagas. It is a revelation to find
that it is possible to imagine real people living in a historical
Los Angeles, from 1880 to the golden age of the movies, making love, feuding, striving, betraying and murdering each other,
raising children and dying and doing the other things people do
in real life as well as in novels. We hear the cries of infants, the
bells of the Plaza Church, the chuff of steam, the purr of pas-

sion. And with people in them, we are more inclined to believe in such vanished ornaments as horse-drawn trolleys, a Queen Anne cottage on Bunker Hill, the marvelous redstone courthouse, the Hollywood Hotel.

It is true enough, however, that even in Miss Briskin's eye Los Angeles was not the jewel of American culture. Her heroine, a Parisienne of station and refinement, returns to Los Angeles from "the most cultivated city on earth" only because of her love for a scion of the novel's protagonist family, the Van Vliets. "Love," she sighs with melancholy resignation. "Love is why I must live here!"

And another Van Vliet, returning a snob from a year at Harvard, to which rich Los Angeles hardware men have always been wont to send their sons, wears gloves on the hottest day. "Gentlemen wear them the year round in the East," he explains to his uneducated older brother. "Los Angeles is a hick town."

While reading *Paloverde* I have found myself referring to *Views of Los Angeles,* by Gernot Kuehn, another recent product of the growing nostalgia for Los Angeles past. Kuehn has collected a treasure of rare old Los Angeles photographs, then paired them with photographs of today's Los Angeles taken from exactly the same points of view.

The change is especially dramatic between "Spring Street North from Second Street, 1885" and "Spring Street North from Second Street, Today." Flamboyantly Victorian buildings stand at the corners of Second Street and First Street on Spring with richly detailed towers, bay windows and cupolas, and in the distance we see the roof and cupola of the sandstone courthouse. This is downtown Los Angeles as the Van Vliets and their friends and enemies saw it. On the opposite page we see the same scene today, all the old structures gone, and in their places the two Times Buildings and the Criminal Courts building to the north, all starkly rectangular in the modern style.

At the back of the book, in a section called "Memories," Kuehn has collected a group of old photographs of places that are no more: The Melrose Hotel on Bunker Hill. The plunge in Venice. Child's Grand Opera House on Main Street. The Hollywood Hotel. And finally, the last picture in the book, a store

front on Spring Street, near Second, about 1923, with a sale
sign stretching across the doorway: EVERYTHING MUST GO!

Most everything has gone.

No other mementos of our past arouse a deeper sense of
loss and wistful regret in me than photographs of that sandstone courthouse. I was a child when it was torn down, but it
was quite the most beautiful and imposing structure I had ever
seen, even more beautiful and imposing than the Kern County
Courthouse up in Bakersfield. It was the color of raspberry ice
cream and had an air of Camelot about it. It seemed to show
that government could be graceful as well as large, playful as
well as stern, friendly as well as just.

It could still be there, of course, no matter how formidable
the arguments that brought it down; and it would be our most
precious antique, a palpable proof that there was an era of
exuberance between the Pico House and the Bonaventure. It
would be a wonder of the West, admired and sought out by all.
But of course it is gone.

Meanwhile, keep your eye on the Bradbury Building, the
Library and—now you see it, now you don't—Angel's Flight.

A TREE GROWS ON BUNKER HILL

"We have a Number One order here.
Don't touch that tree!"

"You do not know me . . ." the letter began. It was the
letterhead of Choate & Choate, attorneys, with offices downtown in the City National Bank Building. It was dated December 14, 1978, and was signed *Joseph Choate.*

It is not unusual for me to misplace letters, only to have
them turn up months later, but there had been an urgency
about this one and evidently I had set it aside for immediate
attention. That had assured its becoming lost.

I started to read it again, with a feeling of being too late
about something important.

Joseph Choate said that his father had subscribed to the
Times in 1895, and the family had been subscribing ever since.

"In fact, my father was a close personal business friend of Gen. Harrison Gray Otis until my father's death in 1911.

"Before the close of this year," he continued, "I wish to get a matter off my chest. I am taking the liberty of sending you an account of my early association and memories . . . a nostalgic reflection of my youthful years. We are all extremely busy these days, but I write to ask you to please sacrifice about fifteen minutes of your time and read the enclosed."

The enclosure was entitled: *A Tree Grows on Bunker Hill:*

"In 1904, 1905 and 1906 I often rode beside my dear father in the horse and buggy, and frequently we went up and over beautiful Bunker Hill, where some of the finest homes in Los Angeles were located. Many of the finest citizens lived in these grand old mansions. Later, the Angel's Flight cable car became the easy, pleasant way to reach the heights of Bunker Hill.

"My law office presently is located at 6th and Olive streets, and quite often, in order to keep myself physically ship-shape, I walk from my office to the County Courthouse for court appearances. For the past several years as I have walked up Bunker Hill, I have thought of the popular title, *A Tree Grows in Brooklyn,* for each time when I reach 4th and Olive streets I can see just north of 4th Street a solitary, majestic, large, beautiful but lonesome tree (I believe it is rubber or magnolia) hanging for its very life on the edge of the cliff with one half of its boughs overlooking the north level surface of the brow of the hill and the other half hovering southward out above the steep embankment.

"That ageless solitary tree is the only remaining evidence of those memorable, bygone, historic days of Bunker Hill. That tree stands as a lone witness to the early California days when one could walk to the downtown section of Los Angeles or the Plaza leisurely in minutes.

"Each time I see that tree I fall into a pensive mood with thoughts of yonder years with Dad, the horse and buggy, the sweet morning air, the blue sky and the clear beautiful mountains in the distance. Within the scheme of so-called progress and development all those grand old homes and the cooling lovely trees surrounding them have fallen in the pathway of the Caterpillar. . . .

"This little story is written primarily to give sentimental

recognition to that tree growing on Bunker Hill, the last and only living, unscathed reminder of those years. The tree was there and growing when I was a lad and when our horse slowly pulled our surrey up the steep grade of Bunker Hill. Presently, less than a thousand feet westward from the tree, is a towering complex of more than fifty-five stories, and numerous high-rise apartment houses. . . .

"That tree is living on borrowed time. Soon it will cease to grace the hillside of Bunker Hill, but memories will linger on in the hearts of some of those who remember the peaceful, serene, azure skies and days of yesteryear in Los Angeles. More has happened to the world in the lifetime of that tree than had happened in all of the centuries and ages prior to 1900—a staggering thought as we look both backward and now forward to the critical days ahead."

There was a postscript: "Since this was written, as of yesterday the bulldozers were operating within fifty feet of that grand tree. The contractors indicated to me that their operations stopped just short of the tree, so it may be temporarily spared."

On December 13, then, his tree was in grave peril. Was there any chance it had survived such a close encounter? I was afraid not. What did "temporarily" mean? I doubted that it meant three months.

I had to find out, and the only way I would ever be sure was to see for myself. I could phone Choate, of course, and ask him if the tree was still there. But what if it wasn't? I knew what he would say. Where were you, Jack Smith, when I needed fifteen minutes of your time?

I drove up on what is left of Bunker Hill.

There was nothing on the ground at Fourth and Olive but a construction shack. Beyond it the raw earth dropped off steeply down to Hill Street. I couldn't see any tree. There was a chain-link fence, but a gate was open and I drove in.

I saw the tree then, just the top of it, rising over a parapet to the east of the shack. It was indeed alone, and it was extraordinary that it had survived on that scarred site.

I wanted to take a look up close, but I didn't want to get myself thrown off a construction site for snooping. I stepped up through the open door of the shack and into a small office where a girl was busy at a desk.

"I wanted to ask about the tree," I said.

"What is it?" said a man in the doorway on the left. He was tall and broad, with brawny arms folded over his chest. He looked easygoing but tough, and I figured he would be the boss. I identified myself.

"Hey," he said, smiling and putting out a hand. "We went to Belmont together."

Tip McFarlin. He had been a year ahead of me, student-body president and star tackle on the football team. What luck! I thought. This man had probably driven off a hundred old-timers or environment freaks who had come nosing around to harangue him about that tree. But we had a bond. The old school tie. Our alma mater was just over there on the next hill, not a mile away.

He was project manager for Campbell Construction, and they were building two sixteen-story low-cost-housing towers for senior citizens. He knew all about the tree.

"We have a Number One order here," he said. "Don't touch that tree. But I wouldn't anyway. What the hell—this is where I grew up."

Actually, the tree wasn't on his site but just to the south of it. "I think there's a very good chance that tree can stay," he said. "After all, it's been home for a lot of good winos."

We shook hands and I went outside and made my way down over the scoured earth to the tree. It seemed literally to cling to the slope in desperation. The blades had cut so close that its roots on the lower side were exposed. But it had a crown of large, fresh glossy leaves and an abundance of green fruits or pods that seemed to herald one more spring. Choate had guessed it was a rubber tree or a magnolia. It looked to me like one of those great fig trees that shade the Plaza.

The bark of its trunk and lower branches was scored with initials and outcries. I LOVE LILY AYERS had been carved expertly in a branch by DAN FROM DENVER.

The tree had a view. To the west and south the dark glass and concrete towers of the financial district; to the east and north the City Hall and civic center. And down below on Hill Street I could see Grand Central Market, which had once been connected with this hill by Angel's Flight. Would it ever be again?

The next morning I got out Joseph Choate's letter and started to call his office. Suddenly it occurred to me that I had found out only half of what I had to know. The tree was still there, but was Joseph Choate? After all, he was almost as old as the century and given to walking over Bunker Hill from his office to the courthouse. In this uncertain world three months could be a long time for a man as well as a tree. And I hadn't heard from him again.

"Choate and Choate," a woman answered.

"Is Mr. Joseph Choate there?" I asked. "The elder?"

"Mr. Choate is out of town."

I gave her my name. "He wrote to me some time ago," I said.

"Oh, yes," she said more softly. "About his tree."

"Yes, I went to look for it yesterday. It's still there."

"He'll be pleased," she said.

So was I.

EVOLVE

"It was the shape of a YIELD *sign, but orange instead of yellow."*

Now and then small whimsies appear on our streets, to the relief of public monotony and the annoyance of Big Brother; but they are of course doomed by one authority or another, and suddenly they vanish.

It is easy to recall such heroic examples as the nude Pink Lady who was painted in the night over a tunnel on Malibu Canyon Road. For two or three effervescent days she captivated the metropolis; but she was an embarrassment to those in charge of public decency and safety, and she was quickly spray-painted into gray oblivion.

A place in history is also assured for those debonair sculptures that appeared at dawn one day in the censored water fountains of the Water & Power building, only to be uprooted and hustled out of sight by a crew of DWP muckers before sunset.

But such phenomena pop up often in Los Angeles, on a smaller scale—tiny anonymous eccentricities that seem to have been created to express some cryptic but poignant message.

For a little while they amuse and bemuse us as we fly to our various appointments; and then as suddenly and mysteriously as they came they are gone. We do not even notice their passing and forget that they were ever there.

Now I am reminded of a baffling sign which I had seen more than once, and wondered about, but whose passing I hadn't noticed. It was a street sign just north of Hope and Third streets, on Bunker Hill. It stood on a concrete island formed by the fork where Flower Street veers west and Hope begins. It was the shape of a YIELD sign, but orange instead of yellow. In black letters it said EVOLVE.

Two color snapshots of this sign are enclosed in a letter I have received from Patricia S. Struve. I recognized the sign at once.

"These were taken at Hope/Flower and Third streets about two weeks ago," she says. "The sign had been there for six months, but I hesitated calling attention to it, as I was sure someone would then paint it out. Sadly, someone did that just this week.

"Since we live in Bunker Hill Towers, I went by the sign at least twice a day, and enjoyed contemplating what it meant —to the person who painted it, and what, if anything, it meant to the people who saw it. Did they laugh? Try to obey it? Ignore it?

"Somehow, the sign seemed to fit Bunker Hill as it is today as much or more than the Tree fit the way it was." (Mrs. Struve refers to the tree that survives on Bunker Hill near Third and Olive.)

I remember quite well when I first saw the sign. EVOLVE, I thought, was rather a difficult word for a street sign, especially since it would be seen by many for whom English was not the native tongue.

Even if one knew what EVOLVE meant, in a general sense, what did it mean in this particular situation? How, exactly, was a person driving south at that point expected to evolve? If you look at the map you will see that by continuing ahead when Flower veers to the west, you will have evolved from

Flower into Hope. That must be it, I thought. The sign was meant to guide the driver who wished to leave Flower and evolve into Hope.

I liked it, aesthetically. "Evolve" is a rather lovely word, just as "yield" is, and I saw no harm in adding a touch of poetry to a scene that is generally all too dreary. But I wondered how it would help most people, since they wouldn't know what they were evolving into. To be more useful, it ought to read EVOLVE INTO HOPE.

That's where I was in my speculations when I received Mrs. Struve's letter. Of course it had crossed my mind that the sign might be illegal—a prank. But if it was, it had been expertly done, and I had chosen to think it was authentic.

For all I know, it *was* authentic, thought up by someone in the traffic department and posted at Third and Hope as an experiment. If it worked out there, perhaps, they meant to place one wherever else in the city a motorist had the option of veering or evolving and might not know which was which. God knows our streets have many puzzling and crucial forks.

But it is gone now and I have not seen any like it elsewhere in the city. So probably Mrs. Struve was right. It was a sport, a foundling, a child of the night, an outcry against humdrum. And like the pedestrian signs in other cities that say WALK WITH LIGHT, it rose above its practical message to please the ear and inspire the heart.

Whatever the story of the orange sign that said EVOLVE, I will never approach that strange corner again without a sense of evolving, and where there is evolution there is Hope.

MULHOLLAND'S AQUEDUCT

"It was one of the greatest speeches of all time."

Los Angeles has more sunshine than history, and its "historic places" are few, compared with those of Rome, Paris, London and even such upstart cities as Boston and Philadelphia.

But there are more historic places scattered among our

motels and shopping centers than we realize, and most of them have been identified in *A Guide to Historic Places in Los Angeles County,* published recently under the copyright of the Historical Society of Southern California.

In a "Note to the User" it is explained that the editors had decided to exclude "all sites of which the only physical evidence was a plaque."

Thus we are spared photographs of some freeway offramp or Alpha Beta market which is situated, the plaque informs us, on the site of a famous battle in which nine Mexicans ambushed seven Americans and the Americans carried the day when the Mexicans' cannon, which had been stolen from a cemetery, backfired and painfully wounded their cannoneer and a small mongrel dog.

The well-known landmarks are here, usually with pictures, such as the Pico House, the Plaza Church, Union Terminal, the Central Library, the Million Dollar Theater, the Bradbury Building and Grauman's Chinese Theater. The editors fail to note, with commendable contempt for recent history, that its name has been changed vainly from Grauman's to Mann's.

We find the missions, adobes and old houses, the churches, movie studios and theaters; but the historic places that fascinate me most are those that I knew about but never thought of as historic.

For example, the Hearst Examiner building on South Broadway, mission-style exaggerated into Moorish splendor; the Shrine Auditorium, which was worth including if only as an excuse to quote Martin Bernheimer's description of its architecture as "neo-penal Baghdad"; the Casino at Avalon, which is said to be the first complete circular edifice built in modern times and which to me, in its setting, is the most romantic sight in Southern California; the Pacific Coast Club in Long Beach, that great fake Norman castle which now stands dark and empty and under siege by modern vandals.

Each of those fantastic structures is familiar to me from my boyhood and youth, when I thought of them as new and wonderful. And now, suddenly, they are historic places, treasured relics of our recent past. What does that make me?

We are reminded that Cole's P. E. Buffet, the oldest restaurant and saloon in Los Angeles, is still doing business in the Pacific Electric Terminal Building on Sixth Street near Main, though the big red cars whose patrons it once served are long since gone; and also that the frame house in Plummer Park, on West Santa Monica Boulevard, is the oldest surviving house in Hollywood. Now headquarters of the Los Angeles Audubon Society, it was once the center of the prosperous Plummer Ranch, which Cecilia Plummer ran successfully while her sailor husband was at sea.

I was not surprised to find the *Queen Mary* listed, though one might argue that having appeared on our landscape only a dozen years ago the *Queen* is hardly a historical landmark. But of course she brought her history with her, like London Bridge at Lake Havasu, and I suppose a place as poor in history as Southern California cannot afford to snub a piece of history just because it was purchased. At least the *Queen* came here under her own power and was not dragged protesting to this colonial shore.

A historical place that is seen by millions every year, but rarely thought of as historical, is the Owens River aqueduct cascade that may easily be seen by anyone driving north on Interstate 5 toward Palmdale or Bakersfield. It appears on the right, a long ribbon of white water cascading down the mountains.

This is the end of the 233-mile aqueduct built from 1907 to 1913 by William Mulholland, at great cost in money and political turmoil. The valves were opened on Wednesday, November 5, 1913. A crowd of forty thousand had gathered at this then remote location, which they had reached by train, automobile and horse and buggy. It was of course an occasion of incalculable significance. In the history of Los Angeles it was the turning point from town to metropolis. But to me that day is memorable mainly because of the speech with which Mulholland the engineer delivered the water to the people. Here is how the book describes that moment:

> After a round of speechmaking, the signal was given for the opening of the aqueduct. Mulholland unfurled an American Flag, and the engineers at the top of the hill turned the wheels that would allow the water to flow down the cascade and on to the San Fernando Reservoir.

Amid the sounds of a brass band, the cheering crowd, and the firing of cannons, the water rushed down the cascade. As the crowd ran toward the side of the cascade for a closer view, Mulholland made a famous five-word speech: "There it is, take it."

It was one of the great speeches of all time. I can't think of another moment in Los Angeles history to match it except when Charlton Heston parted the Red Sea.

21

The Era of
Wonderful Nonsense

THE LAST OF THE BISON

*"The best way to go to Europe is on the
Countess di Frasso."*

My friend Will Fowler has sent me a copy of the late
H. Allen Smith's last book, *The Life and Legend of Gene Fowler,* which is about Will's beloved "Pop," and reading it, for
me, has been like sitting with Will for a couple of hours in the
back booth at Moran's Bar & Grill on Pico Street with some of
our colleagues on the old *Herald-Express* and telling each other
wonderful lies.

Smith's book on Gene Fowler is full of wonderful lies, but
of course they're all true; or if they aren't, they're so imbedded
now in the mythology of American journalism that anyone
who sought to deny them might as well deny the existence of
God, Hildy Johnson and Gene Fowler himself.

I would not presume to review this book as an impartial
observer; that has already been done for us with characteristic
integrity by our book critic, Robert Kirsch; and no one could
agree with him more than I do that the book is flawed by
Smith's own hero worship of "the Last of the Bison," to give
Fowler one of his numerous epithets. Kirsch observed that
H. Allen Smith, a newspaperman and humorist in his own
right, "has to struggle to overcome his own awe of Fowler."
I'm afraid my judgment of the book may be even less reliable
than H. Allen Smith's judgment of Fowler, because, as a newspaperman myself, I was always in awe of them both.

Like most other young reporters of my generation, I asked nothing more of life than to walk in Fowler's shoes—boozing and brawling with prizefighters, scoffing at self-righteousness and pomposity, fraternizing with the sainted and the damned, and, if called upon for such a service, as Fowler once supposedly was, making love to the Queen of Romania on her transcontinental Union Pacific special.

We all tried to emulate Gene Fowler, but something went wrong. Los Angeles in the 1940s was not quite like Chicago in the 1920s, or New York City in the 1920s. For one thing, we had a reform mayor. And though we didn't know it yet, the Era of Wonderful Nonsense was over, forever.

But it wasn't quite the Los Angeles of the 1970s, either. There were five downtown newspapers and they were lively and combative and not always scrupulous; and though none of us ever rented an ocean liner, as Fowler once did, we did some ingenious and scandalous things in the service of truth, and we drank a lot.

But none of us got rich and went to Hollywood (you could take the yellow car) to thumb his nose at Louis B. Mayer, conquer the most beautiful female in pictures (and the runner-up as well) and have our wages delivered in the form of a $1,000 bill at the end of each day's labor, as Fowler did.

It wasn't only that the Era of Wonderful Nonsense had been killed in the war and that dog-eat-dog journalism was dying of the plague that killed off most of the downtown newspapers. The real truth was that Gene Fowler *was* the last of the bison. None of us, that I can remember anyway, was quite man enough to wear his coat. He was a size and a half larger than real. While Fowler woke up from his follies a demigod, most of us woke up with nothing more wonderful than bad hangovers, disenchanted wives and ill-shod children and were lucky not to get fired.

Smith's tales in this book are more than twice-told, many of them; but no tale is so old that H. Allen Smith couldn't shine it up a bit, and the book is invaluable, I would say, for setting the record straight on numerous points of historic and literary fact.

For example, it was Fowler, not Robert Benchley, who spun off that flawless triple-entendre on learning that the

Countess di Frasso, an international siren who was keeping the promising but rough-hewn young Gary Cooper in her villa at the Garden of Allah, had taken the lucky boy to Europe for a bit of continental polishing. "Well," remarked Fowler, as this news flashed along the Garden's bar, "everyone knows that the best way to go to Europe is on the Countess di Frasso."

From my own perspective, safe from the call of flesh and adventure, I believe I would rather have made Fowler's triple pun than to have gone to Europe on the Countess di Frasso.

In his later years, as Kirsch noted, Fowler was concerned that he might die without having uttered some suitable last words; and he did have a fine dry run after a heart attack, telling his wife, "Agnes, don't let the undertaker rook you." Unfortunately, he survived that one; but he didn't do badly, either, when the real time came.

"Are you all right?" his wife asked.

"Yes," he said, and died.

Smith notes that I may have written the last newspaper interview with Fowler and quotes a few words in which I said I felt for a moment, in his presence, as if I too belonged to that Era of Wonderful Nonsense.

I remember also that I asked Fowler why, in his middle sixties, he had joined the Roman Catholic Church. "Why, simply because," he said, looking at me owlishly across his highball glass, "I want to go to Heaven."

If he made it, I imagine there's a lot of hell being raised up there.

SPARKY SALDANA

"Mr. Payne would turn purple, and we feared
for his life."

As his obituary in our paper noted the other day, Sparky Saldana disdained the term "public relations" and called himself a press agent.

Saldana was assistant city editor and later night city editor of the *Daily News* when I worked there in the late '40s, and even then he had the world in perspective, including himself. More than any of us, Sparky knew that life in Los Angeles was a continuous entertainment, full of sound and folly; he loved the show and responded to it with unquenchable good humor.

During my three years at the *News* we had a series of six city editors, most of them on the weird side of colorful, and Sparky gave the desk a balance and continuity that helped to keep the rest of us sane. He was unflappable; he would not be rushed, even by deadlines; he never indulged in tyranny; he declined to take anything too seriously; he never panicked; and he was loved by all.

When I say that our city editors were weird I naturally except the two or three who are still living. Anyway, the other three or four were weird enough for six. One of them dealt with press agents' publicity releases by saving them up until they made a good pile, then tossing them in the air over his head and letting them flutter down to the floor with the rest of the trash that built up ankle-deep in the city room in the helter-skelter of getting out a paper around the clock.

Sparky himself, being only an assistant city editor, was generally expected to handle publicity releases, and he showed his respect for most of them by not putting them in the paper at all. It was his theory that every story that got into the paper was just one more story that could have mistakes in it, and the fewer stories he personally got into the paper, the fewer mistakes he could be held responsible for.

The prevailing atmosphere of the *Daily News* in those days was *toujours gai,* drifting toward hysteria. There was always a great hurry; everyone did the work of two; at least a third of the reportorial staff would be a block away in Don's Main & Pico Bar at any given crisis; emotions blew this way and that with gale force; and the editor, Lee Payne, was given to storming out of his office holding a fresh edition with which he would thrash the air while yelling incoherently. During these exhibitions his face would turn purple, and we feared for his life.

It was one of Mr. Payne's arbitrary rules that the first sentence of every story, known in newspaper argot as the *lead,* could not be longer than three typewritten lines. He believed that brevity was its own reward and also that in coping with the three-line lead the reporter would be required to use some ingenuity, thus producing a better sentence.

This dubious stricture was religiously enforced, since its infraction would bring Mr. Payne storming out of his office, paper in hand. I believe Sparky was on the desk one day when a girl cub reporter turned in a story with a five-line lead. He gave it back and advised her gently that it had to be cut to three. The young lady went back to her typewriter and tried, but the best she could do was four lines. She turned it in.

"That's better, honey," he said. "Now all you have to do is cut it one more line."

The young lady returned to her typewriter and tried again. It was no use. Tears came. Her career was ending. At this dark moment an owlish-looking reporter who was sitting at the next desk leaned toward her precariously (I say precariously because he was stone drunk and in danger of toppling off his chair) and suggested thickly: "Widen the margins."

The young lady saw the light, being an experienced typist. She widened her margins (that is, her marginal stops) thus reducing her lead to three lines, and turned it in. "You see, honey," said Saldana, who wasn't fooled for a second, "I knew you could do it."

On Friday nights, after he became night city editor, Sparky presided over a steak cook in the paper's morgue. Leaving the desk in the charge of a copy boy, he would put on an apron and personally cook the steaks, each reporter having brought his own. These were washed down with abundant drafts of beer and whisky, while the copy boy on the city desk tried to cope with the busy phones and dashed into the morgue every few minutes to tell the city editor what was happening.

During one of these Friday-night fiestas a big brush fire broke out above Glendora, and the copy boy rushed in periodically with bulletins. "Mr. Saldana," he shouted, "it's out of control!"

"Keep your eye on it, kid," said Saldana, turning a steak.

Five minutes later the boy dashed in again. "Mr. Saldana," he shouted, "the fire's gone all the way to Monrovia!"

"Good boy," said Sparky. "Let me know when it gets to Pasadena."

Sparky's poise was an object lesson not only for that copy

boy but for all of us. His phrase has served me well throughout my subsequent career. When the pressure is on and things seem in danger of getting out of hand, I remember Sparky Saldana's injunction to the worried copy boy: "Let me know when it gets to Pasadena." It always calms me down.

Roy Ringer, who now writes editorials for the *Times*, was also on the *Daily News* then and often worked the night shift when Saldana was in charge. "Do you recall the once-weekly poker games in the city room?" he asks. "Usually on payday night?"

Because Saldana was night city editor and in charge, he was also in charge of the poker game. He would decide when it started and when it ended and what news stories that might break during its course were important enough to interrupt it.

"If Sparky was losing," Ringer recalled, "the game would go on until the morning shift arrived." (That would be at 6:00 A.M., if I correctly remember the approximate time of my own arrival when I worked that shift.)

Saldana shanghaied players for the game by giving them a choice of playing or rewriting press agents' handouts. Handouts were always long and had to be boiled down to one or two short paragraphs in the terse style of the *Daily News*. Most of the reporters played poker better than they rewrote handouts.

If a news story broke during the game and one of the players had to be sent out to cover it, Saldana would assign it to a man who was losing at the time. He didn't like to see a winner leave the table with big money.

But Saldana did have to "read out" the copy, or stories, that trickled out from the duty staff when a game was going on. Ringer, however, was never convinced Saldana did anything more than mark the paragraphs, a routine copy-editing practice, and never actually read the stories.

"One night," he says, "to test my suspicion, I wrote a new weather lead that went something like this: 'Tidal waves from a South Pacific storm swept more than 10,000 residents of San Diego to their deaths last night and are expected to take an even heavier toll of life in Los Angeles today.'

"Sparky glanced at it, said, 'That's a good lead, Roy,' had a copy boy take it to the rim and checked his hole card for the umpteenth time."

Sparky Saldana and Matt Weinstock may have been very different men in many ways. But both were true Angelenos, as native to our wasteland, and as typical of it, as the scrub oaks and chaparral in Raymond Chandler's hard wild lilac foothills. They loved the Nowhere City, and they went through life with their margins wide.

About the Author

Jack Smith is a popular columnist for the *Los Angeles Times*, the author of several books, including the national best sellers *God and Mr. Gomez* and *Spend All Your Kisses, Mr. Smith*. He is also a contributor to such magazines as *Westways, Travel & Leisure, Holiday*, the *Ladies' Home Journal* and *The Saturday Evening Post*. He began his career as a sportswriter for the Bakersfield *Californian* and subsequently worked on the *Honolulu Advertiser*, the *Sacramento Union*, the *San Diego Journal*, the *Los Angeles Daily News* and the *Los Angeles Herald-Express*. During World War II he joined the U.S. Marine Corps and served as a Marine combat correspondent in the battle of Iwo Jima. He and his wife live on Mt. Washington, near the center of Los Angeles.